Mirrors, Windows,
and
Open Doors

The Journey to Timeless Virtues

By
Curtis N. Van Alfen, Ed.D.

Printed in the United States of America

Mirrors, Windows, and Open Doors:
The Journey to Timeless Virtues
First Printing April 1997

Published by Young Willow Publishing
Provo, Utah, USA

ISBN 0-9657321-1-8
Library of Congress Catalog Number: 97-60473

Acknowledgements

I am grateful to all who have influenced my life. Through them, I have had the experiences, opportunities, and insights that are reflected within the pages of this book.

My love and appreciation go to my wife, Jeanette, and to our children: Lynne, Brad, Doug, Scott, and Greg, and their spouses for their support and encouragement. And I'll always be grateful to my mother and father for my life and my heritage, and for working so hard to instill within me a solid core of virtues and values that have endured throughout the years.

I am also indebted to all who have contributed to the readability of this book through their suggestions and contributions during the course of the editorial process. To all who have helped to make this book possible, I thank you.

Permissions

Grateful acknowledgment is made to the following publishers, authors, and agents for permission to reprint copyrighted material:

Allison, Joy. "I Love you Mother." Used by permission Ben C. Marker Trustee for the Ezra H. Marler Trust.

Bach, Richard. *Jonathan Livingston Seagull.* Reprinted with the permission of Simon & Schuster. Copyright 1970 by Richard Bach and Leslie Parrish-Bach.

Bennett, William J. Quotes from: *The Book of Virtues.* ("How Much Land Does a Man Need?" by Leo Tolstoy, "The Fox and the Crow" by Aesop, "Truth and Falsehood," "The Sheep and the Pig Who Built a House" retold by Carolyn Sherwin Bailey). Reprinted with the permission of Simon & Schuster. Copyright 1993 by William J. Bennett.

Boublil, Alain & Clande-Michel Schonberg. "Prologue" and "Vatean's Soliloquy (What Have I Done?) from the musical Les Miserables by Music by Clande-Michel Schonberg. Lyrics by Alain Boublil and Herbert Kretzmer. Copyright Alain Boublil Music LTD (ASCAP).

Chapin, Harry. "The Cat's in the Cradle." (cassette tape) *Anthology of Chapin.* Used by permission of the Harry Chapin Trust.

"Keeping His Word." Used by permission of Stan Miller.

Senge, Peter M. *The Fifth Discipline.* "The Power of Truth" and "Bill Russell Story." Copyright 1990 by Peter M. Senge. Used by permission of Doubleday Currency, a division of Bantam Doubleday Dell Publishing Group, Inc.

Schlitz, Don & Paul Overstreet "Dig Another Well." Copyright 1989 by New Don Songs/New Hayes Music (ASCAP) Scarlet Moon Music/Screen Gems-EMI (BMI).

"The Touch of the Master's Hand." Used by permission of Stan Miller.

Towne, Charles Hanson. "Around the Comer I Have a Friend." Reprinted with the permission of Simon & Schuster (from Light from Many Lamps by Lillian Eichler Watson. Copyright 1951 by Lillian Eichler Watson).

"Ujima," the story of the Nigerian village as told by Kouzes, James M. and Posner, Barry Z. in *Credibility: How Leaders Gain and Lose It, Why People Demand It.* Story of the Nigerian village from pp. 119–120. Copyright 1993 by Jossey-Bass Inc., Publishers Also permission is granted "Ujima" (San Francisco: Nguzo Saba Films) as reported in *Friends Can Be Good Medicine* (Sacramento: California Department of Mental Health, 1981). pp. 58–59.

Reasonable care has been taken to trace ownership and, when necessary, to obtain permission for each selection included.

Contents

Foreword   On Reading Mirrors, Windows, and Open Doors   *v*

Prologue   Mirrors, Windows, and Open Doors:
The Journey to Timeless Virtues   *1*

Part One   **Mirrors of Self**   *9*

Introduction to Mirrors   *11*
Chapter 1   Family   *15*
Chapter 2   Other-Directed/Empty Self   *25*
Chapter 3   Mirrors of the Mind   *35*
Chapter 4   Mirrors of Behavior   *43*

Part Two   **Windows of Learning**   *51*

Introduction to Windows   *53*
Chapter 5   Seeing with Both Eyes   *55*
Chapter 6   Mental Models   *65*
Chapter 7   Self-Mastery   *77*

Part Three   **Open Doors To Timeless Virtues**   *87*

Introduction to Open Doors   *89*
Chapter 8   The Virtue of Truth   *99*
Chapter 9   The Virtue of Gratitude   *107*
Chapter 10   The Virtue of Charity   *119*
Chapter 11   The Virtue of Self-Discipline   *129*
Chapter 12   The Virtue of Courage   *137*

Part Four   **Serendipity, Synergism, and Symbiosis**   *147*

Chapter 13   Serendipity   *149*
Chapter 14   Synergism   *163*
Chapter 15   Symbiosis   *173*

Epilogue   **When Mind and Heart Unite**   *187*

Helpful Exercises to Guide Our Journey   *191*

What people are saying about Mirrors, Windows, and Open Doors:

From the moment I first opened the book, it captured my time, my attention, and consumed my thoughts. In my day-to-day life, I continue to reflect on the stories and examples. This book is a must for every individual who wants to live a better life, and to contribute in a more meaningful way to society.

—Paul K. Sybrowsky
Founder of Dynix Inc.
(now Ameritech Library Services)

Mirrors, Windows, and Open Doors provides a powerful model for personal growth and change. Professionals, educators, and others will find this book enjoyable, useful, and full of meaning. Definitely a must reading!

—Lisa Foster, Principal
Star of the Sea ELC
Honolulu, Hawaii

In *Mirrors, Windows, and Open Doors,* Curtis Van Alfen shares years of accumulated experience and living in a way that is easy to read and understand. He doesn't preach, but he inspires and motivates with stories, research, and insightful observations.

—Joseph A. Cannon
Chairman and CEO Geneva Steel

I thoroughly enjoyed reading *Mirrors, Windows, and Open Doors*! I began reading it thinking about how it could help others and quickly realized that the information could help me personally. I would highly recommend book to others as the best self-help book I have ever read!

—Keith R. Halls
Vice President,
Nu Skin International, Inc.

I found the metaphors of mirrors, windows, and open doors effective devices for evaluating stages of personal and interpersonal development. Because the images are familiar and simple, they are memorable and easy for the lay person to understand.

—Debbie Sorensen
Graduate Student
Brigham Young University

This book is a must read for anyone desiring to better integrate "who you are" and "what you do," and, in the process, discover a much more meaningful way of life.

—Craig R. Hickman
Author of *Mind of a Manager,*
Soul of a Leader, and *The Strategy Game*

Foreword

On Reading *Mirrors, Windows, and Open Doors*

During my reading of Curtis Van Alfen's manuscript, a curious thought kept coming to mind: I have not read anything like this in a long time. Once upon a time I did—quite often. Indeed, many of the themes are those I grew up with, in my family and in company with books, my silent friends. As I thought about this, I came to realize that these ideas are not old-fashioned, merely out-of-fashion. Might they become fashionable again?

They must. And with Van Alfen, I think they will. If not, the wisdom and serenity he writes about and so obviously has gained will be the wealth of the very few.

Another thought accompanied this other. As each of us grows older, reference to "the good old days" grows more frequent. But someone in the conversation invariably assumes the adversarial role: "Surely you wouldn't want to go back to outdoor privies, kerosene lamps, no hot running water, and a wood-burning stove. Even those people who embrace the simple life and these primitive accouterments soon become activists in seeking the amenities of modern urban living."

But this is to reduce the conversation to the very instruments and instrumentalities Van Alfen seeks to carry us beyond. The issue for him is the attainment of harmony between who we are and what we do. If dissonance increasingly is replacing harmony, then the relevant conversation has nothing to do with material things.

Except for the degree to which the attainment and possession of material things have taken over both who we are and what we do. It is the resulting unease with this kind of harmony that leads so many who experience it to seek to re-examine who they are and what they are doing—too often so late that introspection is to be avoided for the sorrow it brings.

Curtis Van Alfen would have us begin the process early—in families and schools—until it becomes a life-fulfilling habit, pushing out the habits of outward appearances that ultimately make introspection too painful. The conversation in which he would have us engage is akin to that of Robert Bellah and his colleagues in *Habits of the Heart*.

Dare we believe that such conversation—critical to the context that molds the individual harmony Van Alfen describes—might become at least somewhat fashionable? His is a voice of optimism. And I am at least cautiously optimistic, even in the face of trends that make me uneasy.

The frequency and intensity of such conversation is slowly rising in and from many quarters. Bellah and his colleagues have extended their interests in the individual to consideration of *The Good Society*. Nel Noddings and Donna Kerr are not alone in pushing forward with a philosophy of caring. Jane Roland Martin is a kindred spirit in her advocacy of *The Schoolhome*. Seymour Sarason writes passionately about what he terms, "the loss of the sacred," and what we need to do to find it in all aspects of our lives. And people of all walks of life, all levels of affluence, and all or no religions long and search for that something more meaningful "at the center."

What Curtis Van Alfen has written is refreshingly different from most of what I now read that is kindred to it. Much more like what I read years ago in "the good old days." Much of what I read then has stuck with me—sometimes so literally that I wanted to shake it off to spare me feelings of guilt. But of course, guilt is something one's lifestyle is supposed to spare one entirely.

No guilt comes with reading what Curtis Van Alfen has written. Just determination to work a little harder at what our most hard-nosed introspection tells us is necessary to the fulfilling life in a just and caring society.

—John I. Goodlad

John I. Goodlad is director of the Center for Educational Renewal at the University of Washington, and is president of the independent Institute for Educational Inquiry. He has authored or co-authored more than 25 books. His research and scholarship was recognized in 1993 with the American Educational Research Association Award for Distinguished Contributions to Educational Research.

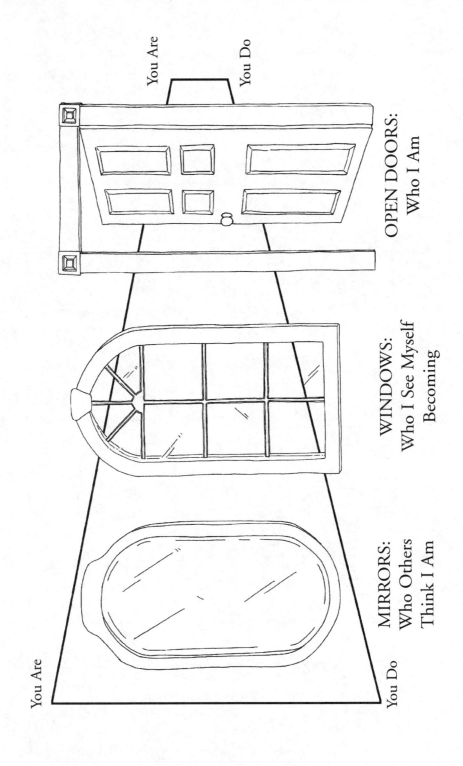

You Are

You Do

OPEN DOORS:
Who I Am

WINDOWS:
Who I See Myself
Becoming

MIRRORS:
Who Others
Think I Am

You Are

You Do

Prologue:

The Journey to Timeless Virtues

"Into the hands of every individual is given a marvelous power for good or for evil—the silent, unconscious, unseen influence of his life."

—William George Jordan

As we begin our association together through the pages of this book, I would like you to join me in thinking through an exercise (no, you don't have to put on your sweat suit and jogging shoes; it's not that kind of exercise). Think for a moment about the people who have had the most constructive influence on you during the course of your life—friends, family members, teachers, business associates, religious leaders, and others. Select three of these people and focus all of your attention on them. Consider their strengths and weaknesses, their attitudes and actions. Taking all of that into account, try to determine one or two characteristics or traits that caused you to be influenced by these individuals in a positive way.

What you have just created, to a certain extent, is your own unique mental model of the most compelling character traits of influential people. As you think about these qualities, my guess is you'll discover that those traits tend to result more from who the individual *is* rather than what they *do*. Indeed, most of what these influential people did was simply an interpersonal manifestation of who and what they really were within themselves. And because of who they were, in some way they were able to create a relationship of trust with you, therefore they were able to influence your life beneficially.

1

It's that way for all of us. We can become people of influence—in our own lives as well as in the lives of others—by bringing *who we are* and *what we do* into harmony. People who accomplish this one significant task tend to lead happy, joyful, successful lives. They can look at themselves in the mirror and see essentially positive things. While they are aware of their own imperfections (and we all have them), they know that they have substance and that they are worthy of respect. They are so at peace within themselves that they can step beyond themselves and reach out to others with energy and caring.

We've just described, to one degree or another, the three influential people you were thinking about, haven't we?

So how do we become such people?

That's what this book is about. It draws upon my years of teaching, counseling, leading, and parenting, integrating personal experience with the results of my research and study in the fields of educational psychology, sociology, philosophy, and theology. It also draws from the virtues taught by wise men and women through the years, such as the profound statement from William George Jordan that introduced this prologue. What Jordan is saying, I think, is the same thing we have just learned through our exercise. Life, according to Jordan, is nothing more than the constant radiation of what a person really is, not what that person pretends to be. "Every man, by his mere living, is radiating sympathy or sorrow, or morbidness, or cynicism, or happiness, or hope, or any of a hundred other qualities," Jordan said. "Life is a state of constant radiation and absorption: to exist is to radiate, to exist is to be a recipient of radiation."

As a result of reading this book, it is my sincere hope that you can become a person who radiates a genuine, positive influence because of who you are becoming. Please note my intentional use of the word "becoming" as opposed to ending with the word "are." While some naturally possess the qualities required to influence others in a beneficial way, most of us will have to make some changes and adjustments in our way of thinking and behaving in order to extend that influence. That means we have to escape some natural tendencies and inclinations, including the temptation to justify—and ultimately embrace—our inadequacies with the simplistic excuse, "Well, that's just the way I am." *Mirrors, Windows, and Open Doors* is a functional model designed to help us change ourselves so we can become what we're capable of becoming rather than resigning ourselves to what we already are—or think we are.

When I think of change, I'm not just thinking about change as a way of becoming wealthier or more powerful or prominent, because to tell you the truth, it won't necessarily work out that way. But I firmly believe that the mental model we discuss on these pages will, if understood and carefully implemented in your life, produce peace, serenity and trust. And when it comes right down to it, what could be more valuable or worthwhile than that?

The mental model I'm talking about has developed in my life over the course of many years. It began as I began my career in education and became increasingly aware of the constant tension between the individual and the institution. I noticed that the typical result of this conflict was that organizational behaviorists worked hard to strengthen the institution so that it could control the individual. My belief was that the process needed to be reversed.

However, although I believed that and had spoken often of the concept, it wasn't until I was visiting my parents one Sunday afternoon that the model took on a name. My mother brought out a book she thought I would enjoy: *On Being a Real Person,* written by Harry Emerson Fosdick, a Presbyterian minister in New York in the early 1900s. Within that book I read a statement that impressed me:

> A person completely wrapped up in himself makes a small package. The great day comes when a man begins to get himself off his hands. He had lived, let us say, in a mind like a room surrounded by mirrors. Every way he turned he saw himself. Now, however, some of his mirrors change to windows. He can see through them to objective outlooks that challenge his interests. He begins to get out of himself—no longer the prisoner of self-reflections but a free man in a world where persons, causes, truths and values exist, worthwhile for their own sakes. Thus to pass from a mirror mind to a mind with windows is an essential element in the development of a real personality. Without that experience no one ever achieves a meaningful life.

This serendipitous discovery gave me the mental model for Mirrors and Windows. Later that same day while reading in the New Testament book of Revelation, I stumbled upon this phrase: "Behold, I have set before thee an open door, and no one can shut it" (Revelation 3:8). My quest for a mental model was satisfied. The mental model as a process of becoming—Mirrors, Windows, and Open Doors—felt good.

As I continued my quest I found two other statements that appealed to me. Flora Whittlemore said, "Doors are interesting; they open, they close. And the doors we open and close each day decide the lives we live." The second quote by philosopher and writer J. Krishnamurti is equally powerful: "In one's self lies the whole world and if you know how to look and learn, then the door is there and the key is in your hand. Nobody on earth can give you either the key or the door to open, except yourself."

So I created from these statements my present conceptualization of our mental model: "Mirrors, Windows, and Open Doors."

Of course, I haven't always understood these concepts myself. When I started my career as an educator, I was assigned to a large high school as a teacher, counselor and administrator. With the fervent zeal of the freshly educated, I scrupulously implemented the theories I had been taught by some of the best academicians in the field. I had the privilege of working in one of America's most progressive, innovative school systems with an acclaimed leader who I admired (and continue to admire) for his courage and foresight. We studied new and innovative techniques and followed the latest research findings to the letter. We took the advice and counsel of the leading social scientists and educators in the country. We were dedicated and hard-working.

And yet, after seven years of dynamic effort on the part of many dedicated educators in our school district, a study performed by a noted researcher indicated that all of our elaborate plans and techniques made "no significant difference" in the lives of our students. The things that really did make a difference were almost impossible to quantify statistically, but it was clear that they had something to do with individual relationships between the individual students and others, including administrators, teachers, and other students.

But what exactly were those undefinable elements of success? And what does it take to make a meaningful positive difference in your own life and in the lives of others? This has been my quest: to find answers to those questions as I continued to learn and grow as an educator and social scientist. Once while I was musing over these questions with a fellow educator whose opinions and insights I have long respected, I was interested to hear her compare our shared quest for interpersonal enlightenment to a Zen quote that states: "Walker, there is no road. The road is made by walking."

My colleague thought about the quote for a few moments, then added: "Maybe we've been spending too much time creating roads for our students rather than giving them models to guide decisions so they can find their own way in life."

So this book is not a road map. If anything, it is a mental model by which you can chart your course toward *becoming* a person, not just *being* a person.

I hope that doesn't sound like I'm suggesting you adopt a façade or become false or phony, because nothing could be further from the truth. Years ago, I took a class from a noted social psychologist. In discussing the principles of growth in human behavior, she said something that has always remained with me.

"Before any of these principles will influence another person," she said, "the teacher must be *authentic*."

I thought that was an interesting word to use in that context, so after the class period was over I asked her about it. Her response: "Look it up!" (Don't you just hate teachers who make their students assume some of the responsibility for learning?) I went to my dictionary and found words like "genuine," "real," "trustworthy" and "true" used to describe authenticity. Armed with that information, even I could figure out what my instructor was trying to say: that an *authentic* person is one who can build relationships of trust through being genuine and reliable. And that can happen only when *who you are* and *what you do* is in harmony in your life.

"So what you're saying," I said to my instructor at our next meeting, "is that each of us is either *authentic* or *unauthentic,* based on how our actions align with our character."

"It isn't that easy," she said. "Authenticity is a journey, not a destination. We are all in the process of becoming."

I waited for her to finish her sentence. But she allowed that word—"becoming"—to dangle until its full meaning became apparent. We are all works in progress. While some have moved further along the road toward authenticity than others, we all experience moments of authenticity and as well as less authentic moments. It is all part of the process. It is all part of . . . becoming.

In this book we will consider how we become more authentic as people and experience greater harmony between *who we are* and *what we do* as we journey through three stages of living: the Mirrors stage, the Windows stage, and the Open Doors stage. We will begin by discussing the Mirrors stage, when we are focused on doing what others expect us to do, and our lives are spent behaving not as we value, but as others value. And if that sounds shallow and unfulfilling . . . well, it is. While it is true that living a life through Mirrors affords the easy comfort that comes from abdicating personal responsibility for our lives to other people and circumstances, it is also incredibly stressful to feel trapped between the expectations of others and the inherent longing of the inner self to emerge and grow independent of outside influences. The emotional dissonance that we experience in this stage can be frustrating and painful.

We are ready to break out of the Mirrors stage when we begin to care less about what others expect of us and more about who we see ourselves becoming. This is when we enter the Windows stage. As you will see, it is a most important stage during which we begin to see the advantages of working with others without allowing ourselves to be dominated or controlled by them. It is also a time of dynamic personal growth through learning. As we discuss the implications of the Windows stage, we will study the process of becoming a person of hope and vision. We will also explore the power of stories to teach the basic virtues necessary to enter into this process, as well as to move on to the next level.

Even the most enlightened people must journey through the Mirrors and Windows stages before they can enter the final stage of growth, which I call Open Doors. In later chapters you will learn more about this stage of life. It is a satisfying stage, when past, present, and future come together to make today a better day. It is also a stage when *who we are* is in absolute harmony with *what we do,* a time when life is dominated by the virtues of truth, gratitude, charity, self-discipline, and courage. We are able to get a more accurate reading of *who we are* because our thoughts and actions are consistent with our virtues. We don't send out confusing signals through behaviors that are motivated by the expectations of others and external circumstances. Those who observe us trust us because *who we are* and *what we do* is seen by them as being one and the same.

In addition to discussing the personal growth made possible through studying the mental model of Mirrors, Windows, and Open Doors, we will also discuss three concepts that can bring our individual growth into strengthened relationship with others for the benefit of mankind. "Serendipity," we will learn, refers to the positive events that tend to happen when we expect more good than bad in life and stick with what we're doing when the going gets tough. "Synergism" represents the ability of like-minded people to join forces to create a functional unit that is stronger than the sum of its individual parts. And "symbiosis" is the ability of "Open Doors" people to come together for the benefit of all, despite their deepest differences. All three of these concepts are important to us in our journey to authenticity.

When it comes right down to it, that's really what this book is about—a journey. But then again, not really a journey at all, because everything we're going to be talking about is already happening within us to one degree or another. In other words, I'm not going to be asking you to become anything that isn't already a part of you. You're going to become a person, but it will be an *authentic* person—nothing contrived, nothing fake, nothing manipulated. And an *authentic* person is a trustworthy, reliable, genuine, *real* person. An *authentic* person is not false or copied. An *authentic* person is one of sound moral principle, which is always—always— underscored with honesty, sincerity, and integrity.

Does that sound like you? Well, it is. It's within each of us to become all of those things and more. That's the goal of this book: to provide a mental model that can help us become that *authentic* person that we are capable of becoming, and that we are even now in the process of becoming.

I should warn you, however, that it won't necessarily happen easily or quickly. You will learn that like people themselves, authenticity matures and grows. At each stage we will engage in a dynamic—and sometimes a little frightening—struggle within ourselves. One of the principles you will quickly learn is; the wider the gap between our behavior and our image of ourselves, the more stress, anxiety, and hypocrisy we create in our lives. But, as that gap narrows, the more serene, calm, and *authentic* we become.

And so we are embarking upon an incredible journey—a journey within. I offer this book as a model that can help guide us to the point at which *who we are* and *what we do* converge and the person we are capable of becoming becomes truly, authentically us.

Are you ready to begin? I am! We'll start by looking into a few mirrors—the Mirrors of Self.

Part One:

You Are

Mirrors of Self

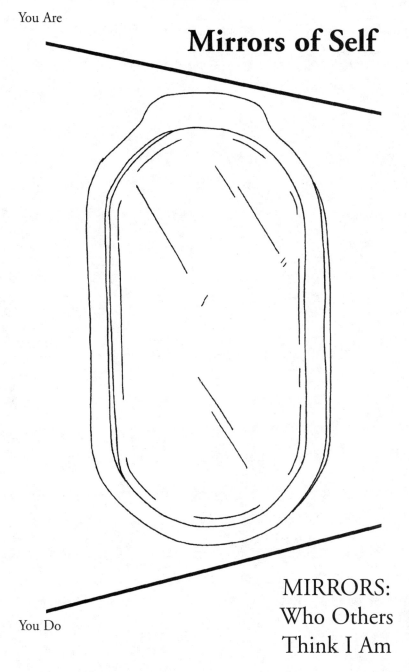

MIRRORS:
Who Others
Think I Am

You Do

Introduction to Mirrors

He who knows others is clever; he who knows himself is enlightened.

—Lao-tse

During a family visit some time ago, I happened to come upon one of my grandchildren exploring the vast, uncharted territory that is her Grandma and Grandpa's house. This was not her first visit to our home, of course, but it was the first time she had been there since she started crawling, and there was a whole new world to be investigated from her unique new vantage point 12 inches above the floor. It was fun to watch her crawl from place to place, thoroughly investigating every inch along the way. Occasionally I had to intervene, such as when she started stretching a pudgy finger toward the electrical outlet or when she found an old piece of lint-covered Christmas candy underneath the couch. But for the most part I just let her ramble, and we both enjoyed the journey.

My favorite part of the adventure was when she discovered our full-length mirror. At first she seemed startled by her reflected image, and she pulled back cautiously. Then she became curious, tentatively reaching out to touch the toddler in the mirror. Then she became enchanted by what she was seeing, and she laughed and squealed excitedly as she played with her new-found friend. At length she grew tired of the diversion—after all, there's only so much you can do with a two-dimensional image—and she was ready to move on to new amusements and wonders.

What my granddaughter experienced on her first independent journey through our house is a lot like what we all experience as we take those first tenuous, uncertain steps along the road that leads to authenticity. In this early stage, which I call the Mirrors stage, we get our first peek at the factors that influence our development as individuals. Some of what we discover here may prove to be a little startling. Some of it may arouse our curiosity and enchant us—so much so that there are those among us who never choose to move away from Mirrors living. But eventually, many of us discover that there is only so much you can do as an individual stuck in the Mirrors stage, and we look for a way to move on to new stages of living.

Still, there is much to learn in the Mirrors stage. No matter how you look at it, individual strength is the key to the strength of society. According to Socrates, "know thyself" was the first step toward successful humanity. "The greatest journey is the journey within," said another philosopher, "and the reward lies not so much in the destination, but in the journey itself."

Defining "self" can be complex. For our purposes I will define "self" as a product of two forces in our lives: the individual's unique consciousness and the social context in which people find themselves. Within this definition we consider the power of the individual to make choices within the context of the social milieu. It also takes into account the thoughts, feelings, and resulting actions regarding the goals and values that the individual follows. Behavior, then, is a mirror of valuing.

The concept becomes problematic, however, as we try to negotiate the narrow channel that separates "self-awareness" and "self-importance." For years students of human development have referred to this stage with such designations as "the other-directed self" and "the empty self," indicating levels of superficiality and selfishness that seem to dominate here.

We are now entering an era when researchers and writers are telling us that people seem to want to move from the post-World War II "other-directed empty self" to a self that is value-filled. By "other-directed empty self" I mean the self that seeks to be continually nurtured by outside sources and influence—consumer goods, calories, experiences, romantic partners, and empathetic therapists—rather than by finding peace and happiness within oneself. The value-filled revolution focuses on the power of one individual to make a difference in the world and an inner power to restore faith and optimism. This revolution requires an understanding of the development of a fulfilled self. It also requires a belief that one individual can make a difference, and that individuals can become what they want to become and can influence the lives of others in so doing.

Based on this belief, Chapter One will prompt us to look at our "self" in the mirror of the family, the basic institution in which most people live and learn. The latest information in the social sciences points to the decline of the family as the basis of the decline of virtue-guided behavior.

Following our discussion of the family as a reflection of mirrors of self we will move in Chapter Two into a look in the mirror of self that is reflected in our relationships with others. This discussion will help us to see how we are controlled by others, or if we have relationships that allow us to work with others. The relationships of self and others have been recorded for centuries as the primary influence outside the family.

In Chapter Three we will look into the mirrors of our minds— thoughts. The way we think is the way we behave. If we are to enter into a process of *becoming* through reading this book, how we think and what we think becomes a critical study for us.

The final chapter in this section, Chapter Four, looks into the mirror of behavior as it relates to our view of self. In order to be *authentic* and to be able to build relationships of trust we must bring *who we are* into greater harmony with *what we do*. When there is distance between these two elements in our lives we have difficulty creating trust. Therefore we must look into the mirrors of self and see the influences on our behavior to understand if we are controlled by others and by outside circumstances or if we are developing the virtues necessary to cause us to believe we can make a difference.

Chapter One:

Family

"The most basic culture in which we develop is the culture of our family, and our parents are its cultural leaders."

—Scott Peck

Debbie and Lance stood outside the hospital nursery admiring the handsome bundle of baby boy that was their firstborn. To hear them talk, one would think that they were the first young couple in history to pull off the incredible and overwhelming feat of reproduction.

"Look at those little fingers!" Debbie said, almost giddy.

"And his nose!" Lance responded. "He has my nose!"

"Yeah, that's your nose, all right," Debbie teased. "But look at his mouth. That's mine!"

"No way! That's *my* mouth!"

Suddenly, the baby yawned. Expansively.

"You're right—that mouth is yours," Debbie said, playfully. "And so are the ears."

Lance considered the babies ears, which, to tell the truth, were a still a little . . . well, funny-looking, if you know what I mean (hey, your ears would get bent out of shape, too, if you'd been through what he had just been through). Lance gently lifted Debbie's hair from the sides of her head so he could check out her ears.

"Nope," he said. "I'd say the ears are your fault."

The young couple laughed as they held each other and savored the most powerful, awe-inspiring process in which humans can participate—the process of creating new life.

Soon others appeared at the nursery window to pay their respects to the new parents and their offspring: Debbie's parents, who were absolutely delighted at the prospect of being grandparents for the first time; Lance's parents, who were welcoming their first grandson; and four great-grandparents, who brought with them the unique perspective of experience.

"He looks just like Lance!"

"No, he doesn't. He looks like Debbie's father!"

"Actually, he looks exactly like my cousin Rosco. Don't you think so, dear?"

"Well, yes, but only because he's toothless, bald, and wrinkled."

And so begins the second creative phase in the life of a baby boy named Kevin. The first phase, his physical creation, was an extraordinarily private thing, taking place within the sanctity of his mother's womb and culminating in the miracle we call birth. As a result of this process, Kevin has a fully functional physical body, complete with a wide variety of inherited traits and characteristics. In addition to his father's nose and his mother's ears, he has inherited a little something from each of the progenitors gathered for his debut. His DNA has already been imprinted with tendencies regarding a vast assortment of diseases, maladies, and conditions— including, of course, his maternal grandfather's receding hairline.

While Kevin's body will respond to genetic whisperings throughout the rest of his life, the actual creative process ended about the same time he emerged from his mother's body. Which is precisely when the second creative phase of his existence really swings into gear.

Moments after Debbie's doctor declared with surety that "It's a boy!" he gave Kevin's little bottom a swift stroke to induce the crying that would initiate the function of his lungs. In doing so, he introduced Kevin to the simple reality that we are all influenced, to one degree or another, by our experiences in life. In a very real sense, Kevin was born a lump of genetic clay to be molded and shaped experientially into the individual he will eventually become. There in the hospital delivery room he took his first uncertain steps on his own personal journey toward becoming an *authentic* person.

Among the most meaningful and life-shaping experiences any of us will have in life are those that we share with other people— especially those with whom we have frequent and significant contact. The family gathering that took place outside the hospital nursery the day Kevin was born represents the most powerful and compelling influence in most of our lives—the family—and not just because it is the first. Included within a family are countless generations of accumulated experience, beliefs, and dreams. While Kevin's parents will exert the strongest and most immediate influence on shaping his beliefs, actions, and attitudes, it's important to remember that they were likewise shaped and molded by their parents, who were similarly influenced by their parents, and so on back through time. In this way familial influence—particularly parental influence—continues through the ages, for good and for ill, creating a suitable environment for authenticity—or not.

"The most basic culture in which we develop is the culture of our family, and our parents are its culture leaders," wrote Scott Peck in *The Road Less Traveled.* "Moreover, the most significant aspect of our culture is not what our parents tell us but rather what they do. It's not so much what our parents say that determines our world view as it is the unique world they create for us through their behavior."

Parents, then, can never take too seriously the imperative causative role they play in the lives of their children in creating in the home an *authentic* environment—and not just by word, but also by action. While it's important to tell our children that we love them and to teach them by precept, they will learn far more from our actions—and their *perceptions* of our actions. Let's take, for example, the following exchange between an enthusiastic 8-year-old named Megan and her busy father:

Dad: I love you, Megan.

Megan: I love you, too, Daddy. I can't wait for you to see me play in my soccer game tonight.

Dad: Soccer game? I don't remember anything about a soccer game.

Megan: Sure you do, Daddy. I told you about it just the other day. I'm one of the best players on our team!

Dad: Yes, I'm sure you are. So, what time is the game?

Megan: Five o'clock. Remember? You said you could stop by on your way home from work.

Dad: I did? Well, that was before I knew about this big project I have to finish tonight.

Megan: A project? But Daddy . . .

Dad: I'm sorry, sweetheart, but this is really important.

Megan: But you promised!

Dad: I know, honey, and I'd really like to be there. But I have to get this done first. I'll try to make it to your next game, I promise.

Megan: That's what you said last time.

Dad: This time will be different, you'll see. Now, you play hard and tell me all about it when I get home.

Megan: OK, Dad.

Dad: Good-bye, sweetheart. And remember, I love you!

Sound familiar? While it's true that occasionally conflicts arise to complicate family plans, it's also true that children learn from these interactions. And if this kind of experience becomes the rule rather than the exception, and enough of these disappointments are strung together, the child can't help but learn that:

- Work is more important than family.
- Promises don't really matter.
- Loving someone is something that you say, not necessarily something you do.

And the child will behave accordingly, both as a child and, years later, as the parent of other children. The Harry Chapin song, "Cat's in the Cradle," comes hauntingly to mind:

My son was born just the other day
He came along in the usual way.
But there were planes to catch and bills to pay;
He learned to walk while I was away.
He was talking before I knew it and he would say:
"I'm gonna be like you, Dad. You know I'm gonna be like you."

And the cat's in the cradle, and the silver spoon,
Little Boy Blue and the Man in the Moon.
"When you comin' home, Dad?"
"I don't know when. But we'll have a good time then.
"Yeah, you know we'll have a good time then."

My son turned ten just the other day.
He said, "Thanks for the ball, Dad. Come on, let's play!
"Can you teach me to throw?"
I said, "Not today. I've got a lot to do."

He said, "That's OK."
And as he walked away I heard him smile and say,
"I'm gonna be like him. You know I'm gonna be like him."

And the cat's in the cradle, and the silver spoon,
Little Boy Blue and the Man in the Moon.
"When you comin' home, Dad?"
"I don't know when. But we'll get together then.
"Yeah, you know we'll have a good time then."

My boy came from college just the other day,
So much like a man I just had to say,
"Son, I'm proud of you. Can you sit for a while?"
He shook his head, and he said with a smile,
"What I'd really like, Dad, is to borrow the car keys.
"See ya later. Can I have them, please?"

And the cat's in the cradle, and the silver spoon,
Little Boy Blue and the Man in the Moon.
"When you comin' home, Son?"
"I don't know when. But we'll get together then, Dad.
"You know we'll have a good time then."

I've long since retired. My son moved away.
I called him up just the other day. I said,
"I'd love to see you if you don't mind."
He said, "I'd like to, Dad, if I could find the time.
"You see, my new job's a hassle and the kid's with the flu.
"But it's sure nice talking to you, Dad.
"It's been sure nice talking to you."

And as I hung up the phone it occurred to me
He'd grown up just like me.
My boy was just like me.

And the cat's in the cradle, and the silver spoon,
Little Boy Blue and the Man in the Moon.
"When you coming home, Son?"
"I don't know when. But we'll get together then, Dad.
"You know we'll have a good time then."

Just as in the words to the song, none of the messages Megan received in that conversation with her father was intended. Megan's father really does love her, and he is working hard to provide for her and the rest of the family. But if priorities become skewed (as they easily can for all of us) and parents create disharmony between *who they are* (as evidenced by *what they say*) and *what they do*, children are left to interpret perceived duplicity for themselves, and to establish patterns of thought and behavior based on those perceptions—inaccurate though they may be.

The harmony between *who we are* and *what we do* is a vitally important factor in our growth as individuals. It is through this harmony that a child learns to trust or not to trust; feels stress or lack of stress; experiences anxiety or lack of anxiety in their lives. Each individual's sense of self, personal confidence, and security is based largely on the integrity of personal interaction during the formative years. Children learn to believe that they are liked, wanted, acceptable, and capable from having been liked, wanted, accepted, and successful. And knowing it—*really* knowing it.

The best way for parents to teach their children the concepts and values they want them to espouse is to allow them to see those concepts and values manifest in their own lives. If father and mother respect one another, it is likely the child will learn to be respectful. If they are always looking for ways to help each other, the child will learn to be helpful. If they are kind and compassionate in their language and actions toward other people, the child will probably learn to be tolerant. Similarly, it is difficult, if not impossible, for a parent who smokes to be very persuasive when trying to teach children about the dangers of smoking, or a parent who drinks to convince children not to drink. And if a child grows up hearing racial jokes and slurs at home, seeds of prejudice are almost certain to be sown.

The source of direction for each of us as individuals is an inner sense that is implanted early in life by the family and directed toward generalized but nonetheless inescapably destined goals. As we come to understand this and begin looking into the mirrors of self, we can examine our inheritance and make a conscious decision about who we are.

Of course, there is some danger in this process. We can't rationalize away our own unacceptable behavior by simply saying, "That's just the way I am." Nor can we blame heredity or environment for the things we do. While those influences will always be a significant factor in forming our impressions of "self" in the Mirrors stage, they are only binding if we allow them to be.

The most satisfying situation for all of us is to make behavioral decisions based on choice through looking into the mirrors of "self" to understand *who we are* and why we behave as we do. Sometimes we will find that our behavior is driven by internal virtues we have arrived at through our own thoughts and considerations. At other times, we will find ourselves doing things simply because . . . well, we just do them. Most of us find ourselves in the latter situation—the "other-directed empty self" situation—from time to time. That's why it is a healthy thing for us to look into the mirror of "self" and examine *who we are* as the influences of family have created us.

This understanding of the influence of family in our lives is the beginning of a consciousness of "self" that is absolutely essential to finding real, lasting meaning in one's life. Through our family relationships we experience the core memories—ball games, piano recitals, family outings, and disagreements, for example—that serve as the foundation of our values and the driving force behind our behaviors. And they manifest themselves in a variety of forms at different times throughout our lives.

Some years ago as an upwardly mobile young superintendent of schools I found myself becoming more and more consumed by my work. As a result I was seeing less and less of my family. Seldom was I home early enough to say "good night" to my children, much less sit down to dinner with them or enjoy an evening of activity together. In my mind, I was working hard to provide for family, so I saw the sacrifice of my time as fairly benevolent—even heroic. But my children saw it differently.

One evening I came home earlier than usual. "I think the kids are still awake if you want to kiss them good night," my wife said as I came in the door. I quietly slipped down the hall to their bedroom, and was just about to enter when I heard my children talking to each other.

"Do you think Dad loves us?" one of the younger children said to the oldest.

"Don't you think he does?" was the reply.

There was a long pause. Then: "No."

"Why not?"

Another pause.

"Well, he tells us he does," the younger child said, "but he never does anything with us."

I slipped away from their room without entering. Somehow, I didn't think it would help matters much if I went into their room and was unable to speak to them through my tears.

That night I promised myself that I would do better, and would give more of myself to my children. But I must not have done as well as I hoped. Recently I was talking to my oldest child, who is now a mother herself, and we were sharing some deep and sincere feelings with each other.

"Dad," she said, "I hope this won't hurt your feelings, but . . . well, I don't feel like I really know you. You were always so busy with work and advancing your education, I don't feel like I ever got to know you. And I was just hoping that now, when things are a little less hectic for you, we could spend a little time together and really get to know one another."

As you might imagine, her comments were painful. But I knew she was right. I had been trapped in the "other-directed empty self" syndrome by focusing on position, title, and goods and had failed to fill it with time, family, feeling, and love. I had created a potentially hurtful situation in my own life and in my daughter's. Thankfully she was wise enough to work through the awkwardness to allow us both the opportunity to grow and to heal.

When I was a child my mother taught me a poem by Joy Allison that illustrates this concept simply but beautifully:

> "I love you, Mother," said little John.
> > Then forgetting his work, his cap went on
> And he was off to the garden to swing,
> > Leaving his mother the wood to bring.
>
> "I love you, Mother," said little Nell.
> > "I love you better than tongue can tell."
> Then she teased and pouted half the day
> > 'Til Mother rejoiced when she went to play.
>
> "I love you, Mother," said little Nan.
> > "Today I'll help you all I can."
> To cradle then she did softly creep
> > And she rocked the baby 'til she fell asleep.
>
> Then stepping softly she took the broom
> > And swept the floor and dusted the room.
> Busy and happy all day was she,
> > Helpful and cheerful as a child could be.
>
> "I love you Mother," again they said.
> > Three little children going to bed.
> How do you think their mother guessed
> > Which of them really loved her best?

I thought I understood that poem when my mother taught it to me more than a few decades ago. But today, after many years as a father, grandfather, and social scientist, I really understand it. And it's true: the words we speak have greater impact if they are backed with sincere intent and harmonious action. That's the only way we can become *authentic* people ourselves. And let's face it, becoming *authentic* people ourselves is the only way we can create an appropriate environment for authenticity in our children.

Even the ones who come out looking like Uncle Rosco.

Chapter Two:

The "Other-Directed Empty Self"

We live in a mind like a room surrounded by mirrors, and every way we turn we see ourselves.

—Harry Emerson Fosdick

One of the most powerful scenes in the Broadway musical "Man of La Mancha" occurs late in the production. Don Quixote, an elderly gentleman who has "laid aside the melancholy burden of sanity," has sallied forth as a knight errant to right wrongs and rid the world of oppressive wickedness. He tilts at windmills, thinking they are evil giants. He claims that a barber's brass basin is "the Golden Helmet of Mambrino," and he wears it proudly on his head. He battles to defend the honor and virtue of his fair lady, Dulcinea, who is really Aldonza, a woman of dubious morality.

Although many scoff at his misadventures, he is blissfully unaware of his folly. Nothing dissuades him from his quest until a doctor, determined to bring him back to reality, surrounds him with a small army of black-clad soldiers. The soldiers enclose Don Quixote in a circle that grows ever tighter until, on a cue from the doctor, they turn their shields toward him. Instead of protective metal on the face of the shields, there are only mirrors. For the first time, Don Quixote is forced to look at himself as others see him—a frail, fanatical old man, not the dashing, daring knight that exists in his mind. The sight brings him back to reality so quickly that the shock of the moment eventually kills him.

Don Quixote isn't the only one who has been adversely influenced by what Harry S. Sullivan has called "learning about self from the mirror of other people." Although the key to personal growth lies within us, it is much easier to see ourselves through external influences and perspectives. We become so obsessed with outward manifestations and appearances that we sometimes fail to see the ultimate reality that is within each of us—*who we are.*

Social analyst David Riesman calls this reliance on external forces for the creation of our view of "self" the "other-directed self." His concept holds that whereas all people want and need to be liked and accepted by some people some of the time, the "other-directed" individual makes this their chief source of direction and sensitivity. According to Riesman, the idea that people are created free and equal is both true and misleading. In fact, he says, people are inherently different from each other, and they abdicate their social freedom and their individual autonomy as they seek to become like each other through "other-directed" living.

Psychologist Philip Cushman puts a slightly different spin on the same concept with his designation of the "empty self." The term refers to post-World War II thinking that the "self" is actually empty of personal virtues that drive behavior, and that the "empty self" has been filled by external influences. Cushman postulates that we have become a people searching for meaning in things, pleasures, titles, and extrinsic rewards, as opposed to finding fulfillment and satisfaction within.

For our purposes, then, the "other-directed empty self" is a combination of both notions into a source of external influence that has the potential to have an impact on us in much the same way as those frightening mirrors had on Don Quixote. Thus blinded and beguiled by the idiosyncratic reflections that bounce off of the people and circumstances of our lives, it's no wonder that achieving harmony between *who we are* and *what we do* can be so challenging for those of us who are guided by the "other-directed empty self."

Recently I heard about a confrontation between two acquaintances of mine—I'll call them John and Bill. John is a successful marketing executive who has developed a reputation for doing whatever he has to do to promote and market his products, regardless of the impact on people's lives. Bill is a neighbor of John's with whom he has had several professional run-ins. The two men have managed to co-exist in the same neighborhood and as members of the same church, but it hasn't always been easy.

One Sunday Bill attended the church class John teaches and found himself becoming more and more frustrated as the lesson progressed. Not that John was a poor teacher—far from it. In fact, his discussion of the Sermon on the Mount from the New Testament was stirring. But he was having a hard time reconciling the moving and profound words that were coming out of John's mouth with the way he conducted his daily business.

As the two men walked out of church together, Bill could contain himself no longer.

"Who are you, John?" he asked. "Are you the man who just taught that wonderful lesson about things like honor and personal integrity, or the man I see doing the things you do daily in your business?"

"What do you mean by that?" John asked, stung by the remark.

At first, Bill regretted having said anything at all. But once the remark had been made, he decided he owed it to John—and to himself—to explain. So he did—carefully.

"I guess I just see a big gap between what you taught today and what you do during the week," Bill said.

John understood what Bill was saying. Often, he had secretly chastised himself with almost the exact same words. Still, he felt he had to defend himself.

"Look," he said, "the expectations of the business world don't always fit in with church lessons. I feel deeply about the message of the Sermon on the Mount, but if my business is going to be successful I have to do things . . . well, the way things are done in the business world. I don't necessarily like it, but that's the way it is."

Bill didn't really buy it. And to tell the truth, neither did John. Throughout the rest of the day John reconsidered Bill's original question—"Who are you, John?"—and he had a hard time coming up with a satisfying answer. Was the real John the loving, compassionate man people saw at church? Or was he the cut-throat businessman his colleagues at the office saw? John suspected the truth was somewhere between the two extremes, but even he wasn't exactly sure. The reflections of what others thought of him distorted and contorted his own perception of himself.

Because his behavior didn't reflect his fundamental beliefs and values, people (specifically Bill) were disturbed by the disharmony (some might call it hypocrisy) and brought it to John's attention.

But John already knew. Deep down inside, most of us know when we're saying one thing and doing another. As a result, our reaction to situations and circumstances is usually inconsistent, and we tend to place more importance on the expectations of others than on our own convictions. Thus *who others think we are* predominates in our assessment of *who we are*, and we become so preoccupied with the various mirrored reflections of ourself that we cannot see ourselves except through the eyes of others.

At this stage of our journey toward becoming an *authentic* person our tendency is to abdicate control of our lives to others. Because we are insecure with ourselves, we look for security in acceptance by others. Rather than trust our own thoughts and abilities, we pursue headlong the satisfaction that comes from meeting the expectations of the institutions that surround us—work, family, community, church. We find our personal peace in what others *think* about us and in *what we do* rather than in *who we are*.

Look at society around us. We are consumed with who is bigger, who is richer, who has more, who is hot and who is not, so it's no surprise if some of us find a need to base our identity upon the perceptions and expectations of others.

Eric was teaching psychology at a community college, with classes consisting of an interesting mix of college-aged students and older adults. One of his classes was dominated by Mrs. Bass, an extraordinarily confident middle-aged mother of three. She was a lovely person, but she was always giving long, elaborate answers to every question Eric posed during class periods. Her answers were usually correct, but the way she overshadowed the rest of the class was having an impact on the learning process. Eric's first clue that she was creating a problem came when he noticed the other students rolling their eyes and looking away every time Mrs. Bass started to answer a question. But he became even more concerned when they simply stopped raising their hands, allowing her to answer every question.

One night while the class was studying self-concept, Mrs. Bass was late. Eric decided this would be a good opportunity to try a little experiment with the concept they were discussing.

"When Mrs. Bass arrives," he told the class, "I want the rest of you to listen carefully whenever she answers a question. Find *something* in her answers to disagree with and respond by saying something like 'I don't agree with that' or 'I think there's a better answer.'"

Most of the class was jubilant at the thought. In fact, Eric had to caution them not to be *too* vicious.

About ten minutes later Mrs. Bass arrived and made a grand, disruptive entrance. Within minutes she raised her hand to respond to a question posed by Eric. The answer was pretty good, but Eric said, "Well, that's close. Can anyone give us a more complete answer?"

Another student, one who rarely spoke in class, raised his hand and said something that was totally off the subject. But the rest of the class responded enthusiastically to his answer.

"Absolutely!"

"That's right!"

"I agree completely!"

The class continued this way for about thirty minutes. Every time Mrs. Bass spoke, somebody disagreed with her. And the rest of the class sided with the person who disagreed—no matter how ridiculous their answer might have been.

About ten minutes before the class was scheduled to end Mrs. Bass stood up, gathered her belongings and left the room. As she walked out, Eric could see that there were tears on her cheeks.

"Uh-oh," he thought, "I've really done it now."

He followed Mrs. Bass into the hall.

"Let me tell you what we've just done," Eric told her when they were alone. "You have been part of an experiment. As a psychology student you shouldn't mind being part of experiments."

"But I *do* mind!" Mrs. Bass protested. "I've never been treated so terribly in all my life! You've ruined my life! You've crushed me! I don't know if I'll ever recover from what you've just done!"

She did recover—but it took a while. For the next several weeks she was tentative and insecure in class even though she knew it had just been an experiment. Eventually she began to understand how much of her confidence and self-esteem—*who she thought she was*—was determined by the reflection of herself she saw in others' eyes.

My boyhood friend, Jack, and I grew up in the same neighborhood. Neither of us came from wealthy families, but Jack always seemed to be much more aware of it than I was. That's probably because his parents often complained about how hard it was to provide for their large family. They never made as much money as they wanted, and as a result it seemed to Jack that there was little joy in life for them. No matter what they had it was never enough, and Jack learned from them that without financial success people can't be really happy.

That philosophy was reinforced at school, where the young people with the most money always seemed to be more popular and seemed to have more opportunities—and more fun. Because he had to work after school to help his family he wasn't able to play football or participate in many other extracurricular activities, and that made him feel even more "out of it." When Jack's father was disabled in a work-related accident he took on a second job to help meet the mounting expenses, eliminating what little social life he had left.

By the time he graduated from high school, Jack was completely obsessed by the desire to acquire wealth. And not just modest wealth. Jack vowed to accumulate a great fortune, for he was sure that the more money you had the happier and more secure and fulfilled you would be.

Because he had learned how to work long and hard, Jack was able to diligently work his way through college. It took him six years, but he graduated with honors and gained admittance to the Harvard Business School. Within two years he earned his MBA and went to work for an international real estate development firm that promised to make him a millionaire by the time he was thirty-five. With his characteristic determination and grit (not to mention enough 15- and 16-hour days to put even the most avid workaholic to shame) he accomplished that goal and more by the time he was thirty. He was regularly cited as the example of how junior associates should function. Quickly he became a senior officer. Then an executive. Eventually he became president of the company.

Along the way he met and married Joanna, a colleague who was just as devoted to the pursuit of fiscal superiority as he was. Together they began to amass a considerable fortune, which only served to further fuel his passion for wealth.

Five years after their marriage Joanna left the firm. With their financial security assured, Joanna began looking beyond the accumulation of money for purpose and meaning in life. After their first child was born, her experiences as a mother and full-time homemaker brought new insights and ideals clearly into view. She began to perceive the world differently, with a new set of values and priorities. During the next ten years two more children joined the family, and Joanna became more committed to rearing her children as *authentic* people and less concerned with things like money, material possessions, and living up to the expectations of others.

Unfortunately, Jack didn't share her new understanding. He was the same old Jack—absolutely convinced that the best thing he could do for Joanna and his family was to continue making more and more money. When Joanna pressed for more emotional intimacy from Jack for herself and for their children, he was either unable or unwilling to provide it. Eventually Jack and Joanna became estranged from each other as they moved in different directions to pursue their respective goals, dreams, and ambitions.

It wasn't until they had to check their 15-year-old son into a detoxification program to help him overcome his alcohol and drug dependency that Jack began to realize that something was missing from his life. Something important. For the first time in his life there was something that he wanted desperately—complete physical, psychological, and emotional health for his son—that no amount of money could buy. Jack had amassed a fortune, and yet he was frightened, unhappy, discontent, and unfulfilled—all the things he had experienced in high school and had attributed to his family's poverty.

Obviously, wealth wasn't the answer. It took an intense personal crisis like his son's substance abuse to help Jack learn that no external influence—money, fame, prestige, or the opinion of others—can remedy issues that begin within. Eventually Jack came to understand that happiness, peace, contentment, and fulfillment don't come from floating to artificial heights on the wings of pretense and perception. Rather, they come from being authentically anchored to the bedrock of the soul, the depths of which can only be reached when we know who we really are.

The tradition of "other-directed empty self" living has been with us throughout recorded time. You can see it clearly in the chronicled events of history, in ancient myths and legends and in the accumulated stories of literature. Everywhere the lessons of focus on "other-directed" virtues are well-documented.

In *The Book of Virtues*, Dr. William J. Bennett re-tells Leo Tolstoy's classic tale, "How Much Land Does a Man Need?" The story tells of the peasant Pahon, who worked hard and honestly for his family but had no land of his own. He was so poor, he didn't think he would ever have any property of his own until one wonderful day when the opportunity to purchase 20 acres of good land came his way. Through hard work and sacrifice, he was soon able to pay off the debt he incurred to purchase the land. His dream of land ownership fulfilled, he settled into a comfortable, relaxed standard of living.

Then one day Pahon learned about an opportunity to get more land. Suddenly feeling limited by his "narrow hole," as he called it, he sold his land and moved his family to a larger plot of ground. But once again he grew restless, and when a passing land dealer told him of another opportunity to obtain more land for almost nothing. "All you have to do," the land dealer said, "is make friends with the chief leader of the people."

"If I can get more than ten times as much land as I have now," Pahon reasoned, "I must try."

Pahon went with gifts to meet the chief. After distributing his gifts and making friends with the chief, Pahon spoke of his desire to buy land.

"We sell it by the day," the chief said. "As much land as you can travel around on your feet in a day is yours, and the price is one thousand rubles per day."

The deal was almost too good to be true. "But in a day," said Pahon, "you can get around a large piece of land."

The chief laughed. "It will be yours," he assured his guest. "But there is one condition: if you don't return on the same day to the spot where you started, your money is lost."

Pahon was delighted to accept the condition. So at daybreak the next day Pahon, the chief and his followers met, and the chief placed his hat at the beginning point. Excitedly, Pahon gazed in all directions at the beautiful virgin land before him.

Pahon began with a measured step, neither too fast nor too slow. As the day progressed he changed directions and he walked a little faster. It seemed to him that the further he went, the better the land got. He went a long way in the second direction.

"Ah!" thought Pahon as he changed directions again to make the third side of his quadrant, "I have made the sides too long! I must make this one shorter." He began stepping even faster. He looked at the sun, which was beginning to sink in the western sky. He still had ten miles to go.

"I have grasped too much," he thought while gasping for air. "I can't get back to the starting point before the sun sets." Still, he began running. Though his heart was pounding like it was going to burst from his chest, he could not bring himself to stop. With one last heroic effort Pahon pushed himself to reach the chief's hat just as the sun was setting before collapsing on the beautiful land.

One of Pahon's servants ran to him and tried to raise him, but it was too late. Pahon was dead. The chief and his followers clicked their tongues in pity. The servant picked up a spade and dug a grave long enough for Pahon to lie in, and buried him in it. As it turned out, six feet from his head to his heels was all the land he really needed.

How many times have you seen this kind of "other-directed empty self" living make a difference in your life or the life of someone to whom you are close?

Some years ago my wife and I saved enough money to take our children on a once-in-a-lifetime trip to Yellowstone Park. We had sacrificed to save enough to make it a comfortable trip, but not a lavish experience.

On our way to Yellowstone we drove through Star Valley, Wyoming, where we noticed a county fair in progress advertising free pony rides. That sounded fun, and the price was certainly right, so we stopped and went in. As we entered a person in a game booth asked, "Did you get a free ticket to play our game?"

"No," I said, "I didn't."

"Well, you should have," the man said. "Tell you what—I'll let you play a free game anyway."

The object of the game was to throw some dice across a panel of numbers. The person in the booth would hold up some money, and if you rolled certain specified numbers you won the money. The man held up $10 and handed the dice to me. Since the game was free, I figured I had nothing to lose. So I threw—and I won. Then he held up $20 and told me that for 50 cents I could throw again. Since I was already $10 ahead, 50 cents seemed to be a small price to pay for a chance at $20. So I threw the dice again—and I won again. The way I saw it, if I kept this up I would soon have enough winnings to cover the cost of our entire trip.

My wife, however, saw things differently. She urged me to take the $30 I had won and leave. "Besides," she said, "the pony rides are on the other side of the fair, and they're getting really anxious to go."

But I couldn't stop—not while I was doing so well. "Why don't you take them over to the pony ride and I'll stay here and see if I can keep my hot streak going," I said. "We'll go as soon as you get back— I promise."

Reluctantly, my wife agreed—but not before she warned me to be very careful. "Don't lose any of our trip money," she said as she and the kids wandered off to find the ponies.

I chuckled at her concern. How could I lose our trip money? I was hot! And the promise of something for nothing was so alluring, I hardly noticed when the cost of playing became more and more expensive and my winning throws became more and more infrequent. By the time my family returned I was well into our trip money. In fact, I was down to my last $25. I had a choice: toss one more time or take my $25, my crying wife and children on to Yellowstone. I'm embarrassed to admit that I actually struggled with the decision.

That night we sat in a log cabin just inside the gate of Yellowstone with a big stuffed animal the person at the booth had given the children and $25 for the rest of our trip. Needless to say, nobody was very pleased with me—not my wife, not my children and least of all, me. What I had done went against every value I thought I cherished. But evidently, the desire of something for nothing overcame my more noble desires, and the "other-directed empty self" perception had trapped me—again.

As I learned so painfully, we create our own destiny through our behavior. Similarly, our behavior is created through the internal process of valuing, and our values are generated by our own thoughts and feelings. And no matter how hard we try, that's something we're just not going to be able to come to terms with by looking in other people's mirrors.

Chapter Three:

Mirrors of the Mind

For as a man thinketh in his heart so is he.

—The Holy Bible, Proverbs 23:7

It was one of those pristine summer evenings that seem to exist only in memory: clear, unhurried, peaceful, and comfortable. My father and I were sitting on the porch, talking leisurely about life. There was a long pause as we sat, each of us quietly contemplating his own thoughts.

"What are you thinking?" my father asked at last.

"I don't know," I said. "Nothing really."

"Come on," he prodded. "You must be thinking about something."

"Well, yeah. I'm thinking . . . I'm thinking . . . well, I guess I'm just thinking."

Dad chuckled. "You know," he said, "I once had a professor who taught me something about thinking. He said, 'Tell me what you think about when you don't have to think and I'll tell you what you are.'"

He paused for a moment to allow the thought to sink in. It didn't. At least, not at first. And Dad could tell.

"Think about it for a minute," he said. "What do you think about when you're alone and it's quiet and there isn't anything that you have to think about—you know, like homework or a ball game?"

"I don't know," I said. "Just stuff, I guess."

"Then I guess that's what you are."

"What?"

"Just stuff."

OK, so maybe I wasn't too clear on the concept back then. But through the years I've come to understand its power—especially as it relates to *who we are* and *what we do*. The thoughts that we think ultimately become the acts that we do. In another sense, our thoughts become the filters through which we filter our experiences. Our thoughts, in fact, are the mirrors of our mind. Every act of our lives can be traced to thoughts we allowed to develop in our minds.

As we mature, our thoughts guide our determination of *who we are*. We come to realize that, in terms of our own personal growth, we create our own destiny. Even though we are a product of genetic inheritance and environmental influence, there comes a point at which it is up to us to determine what we will do and what we will be. While our character is shaped by many outside influences, we alone are its author. And our character is determined by what we think and what we do. Indeed, our character is the sum total of our thoughts.

In the mirrors stage, however, our thoughts tend to focus on the aspects of life that effect us. They are concerned about how we look to other people. We find ourselves easily threatened. Our thinking is often dictated by the expectations of others, not by our own internal goals and expectations. The images in our minds are dictated by what everyone else thinks we are—or should be—and overshadow the other mirrors of self. Our motivation to act comes from external forces. Even our thoughts are sometimes controlled by other people and circumstances.

Several years ago I became acquainted with Frank, a very capable young man who was just beginning his legal career in a large corporate law firm. Frank was incredibly bright; he graduated from law school right at the top of his class. He was capable and creative and very good with people. He had all of the tools he needed to be successful and happy as an attorney.

Except for one thing: Frank was overweight. Not that being overweight is in itself a problem. It's just that in Frank's mind it was a major issue and had been for as long as he could remember. Even as a child he had always been preoccupied with how he looked; now, as he began his professional career, outward appearances were an obsession. He had an image in his mind of how a young professional should look. Of course, that image wasn't his alone. Much of what was in his mind had been placed there by film and television portrayals of what he aspired to be. And what he saw in movies and on TV told him that to be successful—*really* successful—he had to look as successful as the stereotypes portrayed in the media.

And so he began responding according to the thoughts in his mind that had been greatly influenced by media imagery. He bought a home far beyond his family's means because he thought it would give the appearance of success. He put his family at further financial risk by purchasing an expensive luxury automobile in order to impress his clients. And because he thought he needed to be more fit and trim personally, he bought a membership to an exclusive health club.

Of course, trying to keep up appearances can be a strain—not to mention very expensive, especially for a young family still working to clear away indebtedness accumulated from college. Even though his business associates and friends bought into the appearances he was selling, Frank spent a lot of time trying to figure out why it didn't make him any happier. In fact, it filled him with guilt. Every time someone would comment on the beautiful car he drove, he would think of his wife at home, trying to coax one more trip to the store out of the beat-up old clunker she had to drive. And whenever someone mentioned their beautiful home, he found himself hoping they wouldn't notice how bare their cupboards were and how ragged his family's clothes were becoming.

One day at the health club he was unusually contemplative. He lay on the rub down table quietly, which was completely unlike him. At last the physical therapist interrupted his trance. "Frank," he said, "why do you come here?" It seemed a peculiar question, one that he wasn't quite prepared to deal with. "Why do you ask?" Frank responded, warily.

"Oh, I don't know," the therapist said. "It's just that it seems to me that there are two kinds of people who come here. There are those who really enjoy it—you know, the swimming, the weight lifting, the working out, the whole bit. They're here because they want to be here, and they like it, which makes this a happy, wonderful, pleasant place for them.

"And then there are those who are here because they *think* they have to be. They're concerned about how they look or their health or whatever. It's like they're here in a panic and they're motivated by fear, you know what I mean? There's no pleasure in it for them because they don't really *want* to be here, so this is kind of an unhappy place for them—like a cemetery or the dentist's office or something.

"Funny, isn't it?" he concluded. "It's the same exact place for both types of guests, but it represents completely different things to them depending on their frame of mind when they're here. And I guess I was just wondering what kind of a place this is to you?"

Frank's initial response was almost angry: "I don't do *anything* that I don't want to do!"

But the more he thought about the physical therapist's observations, the more he recognized his real motivations. The emptiness and frustration he felt inside were the result of significant, life-altering decisions made for the sake of appearances, not for any meaningful strides toward soul-satisfying goals and aspirations. His thoughts, when he didn't have to think, were thoughts of external expectations and rewards. Like so many of his colleagues and associates, Frank was spending far too much time in front of the mirror of *who others think I am* and not spending enough time in front of the mirror of *who I see myself becoming.* Frank had allowed the thoughts generated by his external surroundings—the "other-directed empty self"—to control his behavior and, as a result, his life.

While external forces can combine to force us to do certain things, no one can tell us how to *think.* I recently heard of a man named Bud who spent considerable time during World War II as a prisoner of war in Japan. For him there were two keys to survival: doing what you were told and thinking your own thoughts.

"They could put my body in chains," he says, "but they could never enslave my mind. As long as I could force myself to think positive, hopeful, upbeat thoughts, part of me was always free."

As masters of our thoughts we can choose to view life with strength, optimism, hope, faith, trust—or their opposites. We have the choice to believe in ourselves, or to see ourselves as the helpless victims of circumstance. Until we truly believe that we have power through our thoughts over the situations and conditions that confront us we will never become masters of ourselves. It's only when we begin to realize that we have creative power and that we alone are ultimately responsible for the condition of our lives that we can make significant progress toward becoming *authentic* people. For *authentic* people accept responsibility for their own lives and recognize that they have within themselves the ability to change their conditions by changing their attitude.

"Real happiness is not dependent upon external things," wrote William Lyon Phelps in *Happiness*. "The pond is fed within. The kind of happiness that stays with you is the happiness that springs from inward thoughts and emotions . . . You must cultivate your mind if you wish to achieve enduring happiness. You must furnish your mind with interesting thoughts and ideas. For an empty mind grows bored and cannot endure itself. An empty mind seeks pleasure as a substitute for happiness."

Even when our minds are full of thoughts and ideas, when we are living in the Mirrors stage of growth those thoughts tend to focus on the past rather than on the present or the future. And when the past controls the thinking process, it brings with it an emphasis on negative thoughts like blame, guilt, regret, and rationalization.

Don and Judy were in counseling, trying to save their 14-year marriage. Throughout week after week of therapy Judy blamed their problems on Don's failure to provide certain material comforts during their years together. She didn't want to continue living with used cars, a modest home, and insufficient social funds. She blamed Don's inadequacies on his father, who never in his life had enough money to buy a new car or a new home in a better part of town. Don countered that Judy's parents could be blamed for raising her to value a lifestyle that was entirely focused on possessions, social standing, and club memberships.

For both Don and Judy, their thoughts anchored them in the past. Rather than joining forces to look for real answers, they only seemed to be able to find ways to blame others for their problems. And they were both bitterly unforgiving, cataloging past hurts with unrelenting zeal until they were near divorce.

Neither Don nor Judy had taken the necessary time earlier in their life together to work through their expectational variances and to focus their thoughts and attention on their mutual goals and aspirations. As long as they were grounded in the past, there was no way they could experience smooth sailing together in any present or future waters.

Far too often we allow ourselves to become trapped in a process of thought that seeks to blame our behavior on past circumstances and attitudes. As a result, we are limited in our ability to determine our thoughts and attitudes at the moment or to move forward in our thinking. Far too often we give extraordinary power to the past, which always looms as a ready scapegoat for any contemporary fear or frustration. What we fail to remember is that it is only when we move our thoughts away from the past and shift our thinking to the present and the future that we can take control of our lives; otherwise, we will be forever victimized by yesterday's villains.

The simple fact is, no person can move beyond the Mirrors stage of development while focusing on the past. That doesn't mean we should not examine previous thoughts and actions. Clearly we should. But we should use that examination to move us forward rather than to weigh us down with the past vicissitudes.

Not too long ago one of my neighbors asked me to help supervise a 5-mile Cub Scout hike. Soon after the hike began, one of the Cubs, 9-year-old Josh, started shadowing me. Since I knew that Josh's father had died a few years earlier, I was pleased to serve as sort of a surrogate father for the boy during the hike.

I soon learned that Josh loved rocks. Every time he saw an interesting looking specimen he would pick it up, examine it carefully, declare it to be "awesome" and stash it away in his backpack. This continued through the morning until Josh could barely keep himself from falling over backwards due to all of the extra weight in his pack. I could see that Josh was struggling with his load but I said nothing. I wanted to see how Josh would handle the situation.

As we started up an especially steep part of the mountain, Josh's pack seemed to pull him back down the trail. Tired and frustrated, he leaned against a tree and pulled off his back pack.

"Curtis," he asked, "my pack is full of valuable rocks, but it's too heavy for me. Could you carry it?"

I could have. In fact, I wanted to. But somehow, it just didn't seem like the right thing to do. Instead, I suggested that we take all of his rocks out and lay them on the ground so we could compare them and decide which ones to keep and which ones to throw away. Josh didn't think much of the idea.

"Throw them away!" he exclaimed, huge tears forming in his eyes. "I can't throw any of them away! They're special rocks—all of them!"

I put my arm around Josh and hugged him for a moment or two. "They *are* special," I agreed, "but they're also very heavy. And even though I *could* help you carry your pack, that would be against the rules. You see, one of the reasons Cub Scouts go on hikes is to help them learn to carry their own packs up tough and demanding trails. It wouldn't be right for me to carry it for you, would it?"

Josh sniffed and wiped away a tear. "I guess not," he said.

"Besides," I laughed, "my own pack is about all I can handle."

Slowly Josh started sifting through his rocks, selecting only the very best ones to keep in his pack. He discarded the rest—and he survived.

In a very real way, Josh's rocks are like the experiences of our lives. Through the years we gather all kinds of experiences, both good and bad, and we stuff them into our psychological backpacks. If we allow our backpack of burdens to accumulate, we will eventually find it to be too heavy to carry. One of the keys to becoming an *authentic* person is finding a way to sift through our thoughts and choose only the ones that empower our lives for growth. The rest we need to be able to leave behind; otherwise, we'll never make it up the trail that leads us out of the Mirrors stage on the way to authenticity.

In *Beast and Man*, British philosopher Mary Midgley develops the important premise that we must accept personal responsibility for the facts of our lives. According to Midgley, we take those facts to create our own realities. As a result, there is no room for bogus excuses. If we think the kinds of thoughts that allow us to be responsible people, we can overcome any challenges imposed upon us by our surrounding environment—including those destructive, encumbering thoughts that fill the "other-directed empty self."

Chapter Four:

The Mirrors of Behavior

The way to gain a good reputation is to endeavor to be what you desire to appear.

—Socrates

We are an enlightened people. Or at least, we claim to be. Laws have been enacted and wars have been fought in the name of freedom and equity for all people. But it is one thing to have enlightened views, and quite another thing to really practice the principles of our enlightenment. The real test, it seems to me, is not whether we have more advanced views than earlier generations. The test is how we actually behave.

And there is some reason to believe we aren't behaving in an enlightened fashion these days. In *Why Johnny Can't Tell Right From Wrong,* William Kilpatrick cites FBI statistics that show startling increases in crimes committed by children and teens during the last five decades. Kilpatrick also notes significant differences in the classroom concerns expressed by public school teachers in 1940 and the teachers of today. According to a 1940 survey, teachers claimed that the greatest threat to educational progress was talking out of turn; a more recent survey shows drug abuse as the greatest concern. The second greatest educational concern in 1940 was chewing gum in class; today it is alcohol abuse. Number three in 1940 was making noise in class; number three today is teen pregnancy. The fourth most pressing concern in 1940 was running in the halls; today it is suicide. Fifth, sixth and seventh on the list in 1940 were getting out of line, wearing improper clothing, and not putting paper in the wastebasket, respectively. Today they are rape, robbery, and assault.

The systems of thought that have prevailed since 1940 have produced the behaviors of today. During the past decades we have created a system of thought that emphasizes narcissistic values and personal pleasure, and as a result the "other-directed empty self" behaviors have become more and more attractive and acceptable.

So while it's true that as a nation we are one of the most enlightened in the history of civilization, many of the behaviors resulting from our enlightenment are anything but civilized.

According to Philip Cushman in the research study, "Why the Self is Empty," such uncivilized behavior results from an inner emptiness that may be expressed in many ways, such as low self-esteem (the absence of a sense of personal worth), values confusion (the absence of a sense of personal conviction), eating disorders (the compulsion to fill the emptiness with food, or to embody the emptiness by refusing food), and drug abuse (the compulsion to fill the emptiness with something—*anything*—from the world).

The distance between *who we are* (beliefs) and *what we do* (behavior) creates a gap that we call hypocrisy, the distance between society's expectations and the lessened ability of narcissistically wounded individuals to achieve them. In the Mirrors stage of our development, the distance between *who we are* and *what we do* is great. The awareness that we are falling short of society's expectations is a further wound to the self-esteem of young adults, increasing the dichotomy between their outward presentation of self and their internal sense of self. This dichotomy exacerbates a character symptom of narcissism, a sense of personal preoccupation described as a false self that masks the frightened, hidden "true self." Thus even the current dichotomy between expectations and experience appears to be used as a way of constructing the empty self. As a result, one of the wealthiest, most advanced nations in the world is also one of the emptiest based on observations of the behavior of its people.

It doesn't take long on our journey through life to discover that the degree to which most other people will value us is based almost entirely on outward things like appearances and behaviors. And since the approval of others is so very important to us during the Mirrors stage of our personal growth, we have a tendency to adapt ourselves to be whatever it is that we think others want us to be. But if the result of popularity is long-term disharmony between *who we are* and *what we do,* eventually we discover that the price we've paid is too dear.

When my friend Carrie was in the eighth grade she ran for student body president at the junior high school she attended. When she lost, she took it as a personal rejection—not unusual for an adolescent struggling to find her personal identity and sense of self. What was a little unusual, however, was how she chose to internalize that rejection. Rather than being stung by the defeat, Carrie became resolute, almost to the point of anger. With gritty determination, she resolved right then that she was going to be elected student body president in high school three years later—no matter what.

Carrie decided that the reason she hadn't been elected student body president in junior high school was that she wasn't popular enough. So she began changing her behavior in an attempt to be popular with every group of voters . . . er, classmates. When she was around the band kids she acted like one of the band kids. When she was around the religious kids she became very pious. When she was around the girls who hung out in the parking lot, she could swear and act tough with the best of them. She was like a high school chameleon, adjusting her personality and behavior to go with whatever group she was associating with at the time.

And it worked. Three years after experiencing the agony of defeat Carrie tasted the thrill of victory when she was elected student body president at the high school. And she was a good president, in part because she adopted the persona of what she felt a president should be. Still, she worked hard and did some fine things for the students and for the school. No one who knew her then would say that Carrie's three-year campaign to become president was unsuccessful.

Unfortunately, Carrie lost track of Carrie somewhere along the campaign trail. She became so proficient at adapting herself to fit in with others that she forgot herself and who she really was. When it came time to make important decisions in her life after high school she didn't know which aspect of her personality should make them: the religious kid? The band kid? The kid from the parking lot? Or maybe the student body president? Carrie wasn't sure which Carrie was the *real* Carrie, and so it was hard for her to decide what to do with her life.

Eventually Carrie was able to bring *who she was* back into harmony with *what she did*. But it took years of struggle for her and for her family.

Throughout the process of becoming *authentic*, people learn to use what time they have to their advantage. In the Mirrors stage, however, they usually make hasty choices in order to reap short-term—and often, ultimately negative—consequences.

Twenty-three years ago my wife, Jeanette, and I moved our little family into a new home in a new subdivision. Although I'd never had much of a green thumb, Jeanette persuaded me to landscape our own yard. I talked to some of my new neighbors who were also doing their own landscaping, and they told me some of the shortcuts they were taking in order to make the project easier. But when I proposed some of those shortcuts to Jeanette, she balked.

"I only know one way to do things," she told me, "and that's the right way."

So we hauled in the top soil. We painstakingly raked the rocks out of the area. We carefully prepared the soil. We designed and installed the sprinkler system. We visited every garden center in the area to find just the right seeds, plants, shrubs and trees that would complement each other and grow without excessive attention. It took weeks, but by the end of the summer our lawn and garden were prepared and planted.

Meanwhile, our next-door neighbors were golfing. Even though they had started their landscaping at about the same time as we did, they had completed their project in just a couple of weeks. While our lawn was being planted, their lawn was already green and growing.

"Our neighbor's lawn is already up, he's been golfing all summer and I'm still at it," I complained to Jeanette one day.

"Just wait," she responded calmly. "You'll be glad you took the time to do it right."

Not too long ago Jeanette and I were sitting on the veranda of our home admiring a beautiful sunset. Our next-door neighbor (not the same owner who had originally planted the lawn) came over to chat.

"You know, I've admired your yard ever since we moved in," he said. "It always looks wonderful, and yet you don't seem to have to work at it as hard as we have to work on ours. What's your secret?"

Jeanette just looked at me and smiled.

She didn't say it, but I knew what she was thinking. Because we had taken more time in the beginning to create the right kind of seed bed and to select the right kind of plants, shrubs, and seed, our yard has given us years of pleasure without a lot of bother. But because our neighbors had been so anxious to get their lawn in quickly and didn't worry too much about creating something beautiful for the long term, subsequent owners of that home have had to scramble just to keep their lawn alive.

Families, schools, businesses, and organizations of every kind resemble those two yards. While some create environments emphasizing instant gratification, quick results, and short-term rewards, others create environments that emphasize lasting fulfillment, sustained development and long-term progress. Most people in the Mirrors stage opt for quick-fix solutions because they focus so much attention on the *who others think we are* mirror of themselves. They are more interested in how they are *perceived* than in the reality that surges within them, and they are anxious to be perceived in a certain way—quickly.

Eventually, however, harmony—or lack of harmony—between *who we are* and *what we do* catches up with us. It permeates every interaction between parents and children, teachers and students, leaders and followers, and employers and employees. More importantly, it affects our personal peace of mind and sense of inner balance. If we're not in harmony within ourselves we won't be able to find harmony in the world around us. Simply stated, harmony promotes human growth and happiness by giving us control of our lives. Through disharmony we relinquish control to external influences, thus diminishing the possibilities for happiness through personal growth.

When I was a young boy, my father and I shared the dream of one day owning a tall, strong, beautiful horse with lots of fire and energy. Father looked for our dream horse for years. He bought several promising horses, only to end up selling them when it became clear they weren't up to our dream.

Then Father found Duke, a striking blood bay with four white stockings and a white strip in his face. Duke was tall and handsome, and he carried himself with pride bordering on arrogance. And there was a fire in his eye—an attitude, if you will—that immediately told Father and me that we had found our dream horse at last.

For a week we took turns riding Duke in the mountains near our home. Seated in the saddle, you could feel his power and spirit. He was fast, he was strong, and he was full of energy. Everything about him was pure excitement, and I quickly fell in love with the finest horse I had ever known.

My father belonged to a precision equestrian team, and one day he decided to ride Duke during a drill. As soon as Duke saw the other horses he became animated and hard to handle. As the drill progressed through an eight-horse figure eight, when control and timing were most critical, Duke bolted. He reared on his hind legs, whirling and pawing the air. The other horses responded to Duke's wildness with wildness of their own, and before long all eight horses threw their riders. Thankfully, none of the riders was injured seriously. But the other members of the team made it clear that Duke wouldn't be welcome at future drills.

Father and I decided that all Duke needed was a little professional training, so we sent him off with a trainer who promised results within a month. But at the end of the month, Duke was just the same—wonderfully spirited alone, out of control around other horses. The trainer said there was nothing that could be done to change Duke, and Father began to agree.

Before long it became clear, even to me, that Duke suffered from a serious flaw that diminished the luster of the dream my father and I had shared. So when a local doctor offered to buy him, warts and all, we sold him. Within a few weeks, Duke was dead. The doctor had taken him for a ride, which went well until another horse and rider approached from the rear. Duke broke into a frenzied gallop, eventually throwing the doctor and injuring him badly enough to require hospitalization. When the doctor got out of the hospital he went out to the corral, put a gun to Duke's head and shot him.

I hated the doctor for what he'd done.

"Somebody should shoot him!" I told my father, sobbing, when I heard the news. "Somebody should get a gun and shoot that old doctor just like he shot Duke!"

Father comforted me, then he told me something I would remember for the rest of my life. "Curtis," he said, "it doesn't matter how strong or smart or talented you are. If your life is not under control you're not any good to anyone."

The problem most of us face in the Mirrors stage of life is that we tend to live up—or down—to others' expectations. We are not in control of our own lives because our behavior is not based on our own inner values and beliefs. Our behavior is almost completely the result of outside circumstances and the expectations of others.

While we will all spend some time in the Mirrors stage during our lives, if we stay there too long we become so sensitive to outside influences that we lose contact with what's going on inside of us. We become anchored to the past and neglect long-term preparations for the future. We become prideful of superficial things because we don't have the security of understanding the things that really matter. And we become inconsistent, responding to external whims and flights of fancy rather than building relationships based on dependability, responsibility, and trust.

One who is ready to move beyond the Mirrors stage enters the Windows stage of existence. At this level of development, focus shifts away from the *who others think we are* mirror to the *who we see ourselves becoming* mirror, even though we're still very much aware of the external influences around us. As we achieve greater harmony between *who we are* and *what we do,* peace, serenity, and happiness begin to take the place of frustration and confusion, and the mirrors of self turn into windows of hope, opportunity, and vision.

Part Two:

Windows of Learning

WINDOWS:
Who I See
Myself Becoming

Introduction to Windows

Better keep yourself clean and bright: you are the window through which you must see the world.

— George Bernard Shaw

As we move from the Mirrors stage to the Windows stage of living, we begin to fill the "other-directed empty self" with a perception of more than just extrinsic life factors. Rather, we are trying to live our lives according to intrinsic factors that will cause us to behave differently.

In the Windows stage we shift our focus away from *who others think we are* to *who we see ourselves becoming.* We are working at "getting the picture"—really understanding *who we are* and aligning that concept with *what we do.* We are beginning to see with both eyes rather than the limited, single-eyed perspective of the Mirrors stage.

In other words, we're beginning to take control of our lives, rather than be controlled by outside perceptions and events. And that's significant because real growth only comes from gaining control of our inner experience. We gain control over the experiences of our lives by achieving control over the content of our consciousness. Simply stated, we must gain control over our thoughts and values in order to gain control of our actions and experiences.

This process is known as perception. Through our perceptions, we ascribe value to each experience. Whether we do it consciously or not, we experience, we think, and we value. If we are to feel true fulfillment in life, we must take conscious control of our perceptions. To change behavior we must first change perception.

Changing perception is an individual process during which we see and experience things not as they are, but as *we* are.

The process of gaining control over the contents of our consciousness—our experiences, thoughts, and values—involves ordering that consciousness to live harmoniously with self and others. As we begin to know ourselves better and gain control of our inner-consciousness, we develop more consistency in our lives. Therefore we trust ourselves more, which enhances our ability to build relationships of trust with others. It is through that process that *who we are* and *what we do* become more congruent. As John Stuart Mill wrote: "No great improvements in the lot of mankind are possible until a great change takes place in the fundamental constitution of their modes of thought."

How we feel about ourselves—the joy we get from living—ultimately depends upon how the mind filters and interprets everyday experiences. Each of us has a picture, however vague, of what we would like to accomplish before we die. How close we get to attaining this goal becomes the measure for the quality of our lives. Whether we will be happy or not depends on inner-harmony, not on the control we are able to exert over the great forces of the universe.

As Epictetus said, "Men are not afraid of things, but of how they view them." And Marcus Aurelius wrote, "If you are pained by external things, it is not they that disturb you but your own judgement of them. And it is in your power to wipe out that judgement now."

The Windows stage of growth is the stage where we work to gain control of our lives and free ourselves from "other-directed empty self" influences. We do that by filling the "empty self" with learning and valuing. We want to gain control of consciousness, which in turn will allow us to gain control of our daily experiences.

This section discusses a process of learning to gain the vision of *who we see ourselves becoming*. We will consider three basic thoughts: how to obtain a mind's-eye view of life in order to see the big picture of vision and virtue; learning through images of the mind, including stories of history and literature; and self-mastery. As we come to understand these thoughts and integrate them in our lives, we will be able to see *who we see ourselves becoming*. And once we see *who we can become,* we will be that much closer to authenticity, for to see is to become.

Chapter Five:

Seeing with Both Eyes

We see things not as they are but as we are.

— Arthur Combs

One of the most exciting and satisfying aspects of my professional career is the work I do with a private school for at-risk teenagers. Many of these young people are sent to the school as a last resort. They have discovered ways (some of them incredibly creative) to get themselves into so much trouble with their families, their schools and, in some cases, the law that they are sent to us for around-the-clock therapy and teaching.

One such youngster was Diane (not her real name). Although I try awfully hard not to judge people based on their appearance, it was difficult not to jump to a few conclusions about Diane the first time I saw her. Half of her head was shaved bald. The other half was dyed black and coated with a gooey, greasy substance that allowed her to form about twelve spikes with her hair. Her make-up was thick, her clothes were shoddy, and she sent out clear signals of anger and resentment toward everyone and anyone who approached her.

As we began to work with her it became clear that Diane could only see herself in the mirror of *who others thought she was.* She was obsessed with her "friends," and for the first few weeks after she arrived all she could think or talk about was getting back to them. In a very real way she was like an alcoholic or a drug addict, and she was going through withdrawal. Her psychological and emotional dependency upon her friends left her incapable of interpreting the world for herself on her own terms. She could only see herself as a reflection of *who others thought she was,* and she had no sense of vision for herself or *who she could one day become.*

Once the bonds of dependency were broken and the pangs of withdrawal subsided, however, we began to work with her. Caring, loving therapists and teachers helped sharpen the focus of her mirrors of self. Soon her minds' eye began to see through open windows into the possibilities of all that she could become. Where once there was only a vague notion of value based on acceptance by the group, there began to bloom optimism based on vision, hope, and long-term dreams. Over time, we helped her develop a central core of values upon which she could draw in making future decisions.

Thirteen months after she arrived at our school, Diane was ready to head out on her own. Blond, clear-eyed, and beautiful, she graduated in front of a crowd of well-wishers who couldn't help but be touched by the growth and maturity that had taken place during the previous year. The moody, dependent, crowd-follower had been replaced by a calm, poised, confident person well on her way to becoming *authentic.* As she expressed her thanks to family and new friends it was clear to see that, for perhaps the first time in her life, she was looking in two new directions—outward and upward.

And that she enjoyed the view.

"A person completely wrapped up in himself makes a small package," wrote Harry Emerson Fosdick, a prominent Presbyterian minister. "To pass from a mirror mind to a mind with windows is an essential element in the development of a real personality. Without that experience no one ever achieves a meaningful life."

What Fosdick is saying, I think, is that it isn't enough to simply have a view, or a perspective of life. We must have a *vision* for our lives. According to the Proverb, "where there is no vision the people perish." Or, as Harvard philosopher James Allen writes, "The vision that you glorify in your mind, the ideal that you enthrone in your heart, this will build your life. By this you will become."

In order to be meaningful, our lives need to be focused on some kind of *vision* of our life—a hope, belief, or dream. In the "mirrors" stage we're controlled by rules, regulations, and institutional power. In the Windows stage we learn to use our hopes, beliefs, and dreams to shape the institutions in our life. The order of interactions is adjusted so that the dominating notion is *who I think I can become.* Thus we begin to make our *own* choices of *who we are.* We begin to become our *own* person—an *authentic* person.

In order to teach my students the importance of having a vision for living I often conduct an interesting exercise. I divide the students into three groups and assign each group to a table. On each table is a different 2,000-piece picture puzzle awaiting assembly. But only one of the three tables is given a picture of the completed puzzle so they know what it is supposed to look like. One of the other groups is similarly given a picture, but unknown to them, it is the wrong picture. And the last group is told to assemble the puzzle without any picture of it at all.

The dynamics of each group are interesting and revealing. The group without a picture usually accepts their challenge with enthusiasm. Leaders emerge who begin delegating responsibility—sorting colors, putting the edges together first, and so forth. They quickly become obsessed with trying to figure out what the picture is. About a half an hour into the project, however, frustration begins to replace enthusiasm. The group disappears, as individuals decide they can do better on their own. Eventually people start leaving the group, bored and frustrated.

The group with the incorrect picture begins with the same level of energy and enthusiasm. Within about 20 minutes, however, contention begins to develop. There are disagreements over the picture, their interpretation of the parts and their relationship to the whole. Friendly conversation becomes tense and terse. Then, as if in unison, they turn on the teacher: "This is the wrong picture, isn't it?" At this point I usually smile and encourage them to keep working, but they usually never recover. Once doubt has crept in they reject the picture and continue in a pattern similar to the first group.

Through all of this, the last group—the one with the correct picture—is moving forward with lots of laughter and pleasant conversation. Individuals are helping one another with assigned sections. When pieces are fit together, they cheer each other with gusto. They become a cohesive unit—positive, friendly, and supportive. As their puzzle takes shape they start talking about getting together and doing this again some time—just for fun.

The other groups, meanwhile, can't wait to get away from each other. In fact, within an hour or so most of them have left—bored, frustrated, and filled with anxiety.

Usually one of the most stimulating class periods of the year is the one right after the group puzzle experiment. Personal applications abound as class members sift through the experience. Some talk about the frustration of trying to accomplish something meaningful without a sense of direction or vision. Other discuss how it feels to work toward someone else's vision only to discover that it isn't right for us. Still others reflect on the peace and happiness that came from having a clear vision and working together with similarly minded others to bring that vision to pass.

The point is that we should be devoting our time toward the development of an individual picture of our life's purpose and direction. We must create our own "big picture" into which the parts of our lives must fit. Through a process of learning we must come to know *who we are* so that *what we do* is congruent and harmonious with the creation of our vision of life or our "big picture" of life's purpose.

Far too many of us try to make it through life without this picture. Some of us feel deceived because we have been working for years toward the wrong picture. Instead of looking toward life's dreams hopefully, we tend to view the world through a jaundiced eye of sarcasm, cynicism, and doubt. But those who have taken the time to create for themselves a picture of life, and who are working toward *who they see themselves becoming* are more likely to see the world as wholesome, exciting, warm, and productive.

Simply put, as we bring our view of self, our thoughts, and our values together through a process of learning, we have a vision of life that will ultimately make our life worth living—and authentically ours.

In order to visualize *who we can become,* it is usually helpful to develop mental images as patterns. My teenage grandson Mark is an outstanding baseball player. More than anything else, he wants to be a professional athlete. Consequently, he holds up certain professional athletes as the model of what he wants someday to be. He studies their moves and techniques. He practices throwing and hitting the way they throw and hit. He wears his baseball hat like they do, hitches up his pants the way they do, and buys the same kind of cleats they wear. By examining the model of his athletic heroes—both for good and ill—Mark has been able to create for himself a clear vision of what he wants someday to be.

A granddaughter, Kara, is much younger than Mark. But when I ask her what she wants to be when she grows up, she also has a crystal clear vision: "I want to be a school principal, just like my Dad!" Now, I realize that her vision may shift drastically through the years. But at this point in her life, her experience and learning has given her a mental model of a person she loves and wants to emulate.

This is true for all of us. Our vision for our own lives is based on what—and who—we learn to value. As we gain new knowledge we sift it through the perspective of our beliefs and values. Our challenge in the Windows stage of our journey to authenticity is to thoroughly investigate all of the possibilities of our potential. As we begin to develop thoughts and ideas on the subject, this quest for learning and our ability to value will naturally create a basis from which we can make positive choices that maintain harmony between *who we are* and *what we do.*

These visions and mental models as seen through the windows of the mind direct our behavior. They become for our lives what the completed picture is to those working on a puzzle. With the picture as a guide, putting the puzzle together is a fun, productive experience. But without the picture, or with the *wrong* picture as a guide, the same experience can be frustrating and unsatisfying.

So it is with our lives. With the vision or a "big picture" to guide our decisions and choices, life can be fun and productive. Anxiety is diminished, stress is reduced, and our relationships with other people are more satisfying because we find them less threatening than we do in the Mirrors stage. Such maturity just isn't possible in the Mirrors stage. But in the Windows stage . . . well, the possibilities are only limited by the boundaries of the mind.

Perception, the process of experiencing, thinking, and valuing, is closely linked to time. As we enter the Windows stage in our process of becoming, the future begins to play a significant role. But the challenge we face is in finding a way to break with the past. Time also plays a role in the patience or impatience we develop in allowing life to flow. Time itself can be either a chief ally or a major deterrent throughout the process of becoming. If we learn to use our time well, drawing upon the lessons of the past while we use the present to achieve our dreams and visions for the future, our mirrors of self fade easily into windows through which we facilitate our own growth. But the chief stumbling block to such growth is our inability to take the time needed to deal with life's most complicated social, intellectual, and spiritual problems. In the Mirrors stage we feel pressure to respond to challenges in a "quick fix" mode. Our focus on external forces puts a kind of self-imposed pressure on us to satisfy immediate concerns *immediately,* regardless of long-term future considerations. If we fail to take the time to study, learn, evaluate, and meditate our way to good decisions and choices, we abdicate to the fates (whoever or whatever they might be) control of our own personal destiny.

For most of us, the time to take control of our own lives happens during the teenage years. No matter how carefully our parents, teachers, and leaders have taught us their values and ideals, we arrive at a point in time when we feel we must choose for ourselves what we will believe, value, and hold dear. This can be a frustrating time for everyone, especially conscientious parents who see their beloved children questioning time-honored standards of right and wrong. Sometimes we want to force our will upon our young people—for their own good, of course—because we know through our own experience what is best for them—or at least, we think we do.

A friend of mine told me about a discussion he recently had with his teenage son. The issue, he said, was pants—his son's pants. Not that the boy wasn't wearing them (which really *would* have been something to get worked up about). It's just that the youngster was, in his father's opinion, wearing them wrong.

"But everybody wears pants like this, Dad," said the teenager, his trousers barely on far enough to cover what they were intended to cover. "It's cool!"

"Yeah, cool," his father replied. "And it'll be downright chilly if you ever bend over."

"But Dad . . ."

"Look, why don't you pull them up . . . to about *here*," the father said, hiking his son's pants up to the point that was "cool" when he was in high school. He cinched his belt tightly around his waist.

"See? That feels better, doesn't it?"

"It feels like I'm being cut in half," the boy said, sourly. Then he glanced in a mirror—and grimaced. "Great. Now I look like a nerd."

Knowing that the only thing worse than actually *being* a nerd is *looking* like one, my friend tried to make light of the situation. "If anyone accuses you of being a nerd," he said, "just show them your last report card. Anyway, that's why God gave you a belly button—so you'd know how high to pull up your pants." The young man didn't think it was funny.

"Hey," he said, "just because you use your belt to help you suck in your stomach doesn't mean I have to . . . "

"Hold it just one minute, young man. Are you saying that I'm fat?"

"Are you saying that you're not?"

My friend went to his wife for support, but all he got was laughter.

"You've got to be kidding," she said, still chuckling. "Can't you guys find anything important to argue about?"

"Important? We're talking about the boy's pants here!"

"I understand that," she replied patiently. "What I don't understand is, what's the problem? If he wants to wear his pants lower than you do, so what?"

My friend tried to explain how deteriorating dress standards led to the decline and fall of the Roman Empire, the Boxer Rebellion, and Cher, but deep inside he knew his wife had a point. His son was expressing his own sense of style based on his own emerging values. He was breaking with the past—his father's past—in making choices from within himself. His father saw it as rebellion, but it wasn't. It was simply a first step in the important process of establishing individual identity through independent values. He was starting to frame the "big picture" that would contain his vision of life by examining various aspects of the question, *who do I think I can become?*

In other words, he was beginning to see his place in the present and future through windows of the past.

Patricia, a college student, was searching through all aspects of her university surroundings for insights to help her in her quest. For one of her classes she studied Ralph Waldo Emerson's *Essay on Self-Reliance,* which led her to several significant mental models:

> To believe in your own thought, to believe that what is true for you in your private heart is true for all men—that is genius . . . For the inmost in due time becomes the outmost . . . A man should learn to detect and watch that gleam of light which flashes across his mind from within . . . Yet he dismisses without notice his thought because it is his. In every work of genius we recognize our own rejected thoughts.

As Patricia pondered this idea she realized how many times in her life she had come up with an idea, only to let it pass because she didn't think it was important. It wasn't until later, when someone else spoke or wrote the same thought, that she realized how profound her own idea had been. Emerson continued:

> Else tomorrow as a stranger will say with masterly good sense precisely what we have thought and felt all the time, and we shall be forced to take with shame our own opinion from another.

This lesson was valuable for Patricia, as it is for all of us. We must learn to trust ourselves, for our thoughts and instincts have value—for ourselves and for others.

Unfortunately, however, most of us tend to rely on the thoughts and counsel of others. And because we don't trust our own thinking, we don't believe that our thoughts and actions are important or meaningful to anyone else. The potential impact of our life—our thoughts, our attitudes, and our behaviors—on ourselves and others is an important window through which we must look in order to see the vision of *who we can become.*

Of course, this isn't always easy to see. As Patricia read in Emerson's *Essay on Self-Reliance:*

> There is a time in every man's education when he arrives at the conviction that envy is ignorance, that imitation is suicide: that he must take himself for better or worse as his portion.

Suddenly it occurred to Patricia that for twelve years of public schooling and three years of university study, learning had been for her primarily an external experience. Most of her effort had been for the purpose of meeting the expectations of others. Only rarely had she studied and learned for the sake of personal joy and satisfaction. She was working to satisfy others.

Eventually she realized that the same attitude extended to almost every facet of her life. Even something so intensely personal as her religious beliefs was grounded, to a great degree, in meeting the expectations of others. She began to question the depth of her own commitment to God. Were her feelings sincere, or was she just imitating what she thought she *should* feel? She began to understand that in order for her faith to have any meaningful impact in her life, it must come from within herself—regardless of church or family expectations.

In that sense, we all create our own destiny. Happiness—*real* happiness, whole-souled, and fulfilling, not the shallow, superficial kind that comes from wallowing in momentary pleasure—is the outgrowth of our use of time and our willingness to look to the future and the long-term benefit of learning. It doesn't necessarily mean that we will always be the best there is, just the best we can be. And that is enough.

Our journey through life is enhanced if we anticipate the hard work it will require, as well as the ups and downs we will encounter along the way. As we confront each obstacle we need to remind ourselves that it is in overcoming obstacles that we gain confidence and trust in ourselves. Not that the act of overcoming is made any easier as a result of that understanding. But we are more inclined to be patient with life's challenges if we can view them in that context. If we have confidence in ourselves, if we know that our feet are on the right path and we are headed in the right direction then we are more likely to be patient enough to develop long-term solutions to life's problems—as opposed to feeling driven to come up with immediate solutions—*immediately!*

When Sally was in the third grade her school put on a production of Shakespeare's "As You Like It." It was a wonderful experience for the children, but not exactly what you would call an aesthetic triumph. The children wore Shakespearean era clothes, learned their parts, and stepped forward and said them clearly. Parents took pictures and enjoyed the performance. It was cute and fun, but nobody claimed the production was ready for a run on Broadway.

A few months after the elementary school performance, a local professional theater company undertook the same play. Sally's parents thought it would be fun for her to see "As You Like It" as the Bard intended it. Besides, as Sally's mother observed, "it will be nice to see what the plot was supposed to be."

So the entire family went to the professional production. Sally was especially excited about seeing "her" play again. But as the performance progressed, she became more and more confused.

"Mom," she whispered about midway through the first act, "when are they going to do *my* play?"

"This *is* your play, honey," her mother replied. "This is 'As You Like It.'"

Sally studied the onstage action for a few more minutes. "No, this isn't my play," she concluded. "I don't see *me!*"

No matter how hard her parents tried to persuade her, Sally would not accept the performance she was seeing as Shakespeare's "As You Like It." Even though all of the elements of superb theater were in place—excellent acting, splendid direction, wonderful scenery, costumes and props—it was ultimately unsatisfying to her because it was so unlike what she was familiar with and what she was expecting to see. All the way home Sally expressed her disappointment. "That wasn't our play," she said.

Because her perspective was limited, Sally was unable to appreciate what could have been a meaningful artistic experience. All of us who are stuck in the Mirrors stage are similarly limited by a narrow, one-eyed view and understanding. As we move into the Windows stage we become more open to new information and ideas. With a broader perspective, we become more aware of ourselves and how we fit into the world around us. And as a result, we are better able to make choices based on real values of what we believe because we have become more capable of seeing life as a whole rather than in parts.

Chapter Six:

Mental Models

You've got to be taught to hate and fear.
You've got to be taught from year to year.
It's got to be drummed in your dear little ear.
You've got to be carefully taught.

—Oscar Hammerstein II

Back in Chapter Three we talked about a wonderful insight I received from my father. Remember? He said, "Tell me what you think about when you don't have to think, and I'll tell you what you are." That's an important thought for us to come back to at this point. Contrary to common belief, the normal state of the mind is chaos. Without training and or proper models from the external world to demand our attention, people generally are unable to focus their thoughts for more than a few minutes at a time.

In the Windows stage we are on a quest to gain control over consciousness. That is a great challenge for all of us because of this natural tendency toward chaos. This is especially noticeable in group interactions, where external influences are most pronounced. In most groups, activities are not particularly meaningful or goal-directed. Unless a person or group of people know how to give order to thoughts, attention will be attracted to whatever is most problematic at the moment. It will focus on some real or imagined pain, on recent grudges, or long-term frustrations. Entropy is the normal state of consciousness, a state that is neither useful nor enjoyable. For this reason, people in groups are usually eager to fill their time with anything that distracts the group's attention from turning inward and dwelling on feelings.

This explains why such a huge proportion of group time is invested in the pursuit of entertainment, even though such pursuits are rarely fulfilling on any level. Indeed, much of what we see on television and in films is numbing, a teletronic sedative that dulls the mind and distracts one from fully experiencing his or her own life. But Michael Medved, noted television and film critic, has said that while the content of television and films is a concern, it isn't the greatest concern. The number one concern, according to Medved, is the amount of time spent watching television and movies. He points out that the average American watches twenty-five hours of television per week, which equates to thirteen years of television in a typical lifetime.

What does this have to do with learning? Only this: learning is the process of gaining control over the content of our consciousness. To gain control of our consciousness and fill the "other-directed empty self," it is necessary to turn to intrinsic motives rather than external influences. And the only way we can do that is through entering into a learning process that helps us to break away from the easy, "other-directed empty self" ways of dealing with life.

Such learning processes require time and focus on models that can help us to see first-hand the patterns and consequences of our behaviors. Modeling is a powerful way to learn, especially when the models we are observing take place in the world's most influential training ground and among the world's most persuasive teachers—the home and the family.

Recently, in a mall, I watched a mother and her three small children. The children were fighting and speaking harshly to one another, and generally being disruptive and out of control. The mother stood idly by, hoping, I'm sure, that they would stop on their own. Just as things were really getting out of hand, the mother walked over and struck each of the children, and in a loud, harsh, expletive-laden voice shouted at the youngsters to "stop hitting and screaming at each other." Then she slammed them onto a bench and told them to "sit there and shut up!"

Like it or not, she had just provided her children with a model of how to deal with frustration. And if research is to be believed, it is a sad pattern that will be repeated in the lives of her children—and in the lives of her children's children, and their children, and so on down the line.

The fact is, it is difficult to overcome the negative and destructive behaviors we learn through the models we see in our homes and families. Mental models determine not only how we make sense of the world in which we live, but also how we take action. Our mental models provide for us a framework for our values. If we learn from "other-directed empty self" models, then that will be at the core of our values and beliefs. But if we learn from models that reach upward and outward with positive influence based on relationships of trust, then that will likely be the direction of our lives.

During a recent seminar, some business executives were discussing the importance of building relationships of trust. Finally, after about an hour of thoughtful conversation, one young man had had enough.

"This discussion is absolutely pointless!" he said, exasperated. "There's no way that you can trust people—not in this organization or any other organization. Without controls and supervision, the natural tendency of all people is to take advantage. And that's just what they'll do if you trust them—they'll take advantage of you."

I was fascinated by his comment, not because I agreed with his philosophy, but because I wondered about the experiences and mental models that guided the formation of his basic belief that people could not be trusted. I found myself feeling a little sorry for someone who had probably been burned a few times in his relationships with others.

Another comment that similarly caught my attention came out of a junior high school faculty meeting. "Let me say something to the young members of our faculty," one veteran teacher rose to say. "The earlier you realize that teenagers are difficult, the better off you will be. Junior high is a war zone; it's us against them. Don't expect this to be a pleasant experience, and you won't be disappointed."

This expression of one person's idea of teenagers triggered a lively discussion in faculty meeting, which resulted in the conclusion that different teachers working with the exact same children can have widely divergent experiences with those children. I left with the belief that a big part of a teacher's attitude toward students has to do with that teacher's own respective mental models of who or what teenagers are. The difference is what each one believes.

It is impossible to separate the learning/teaching process from *who we are*. A wise person once said, "You can no more teach what you ain't got than you can go back to some place where you ain't never been." Each person teaches through *who they are*. The principle that comes into play here is the power of self as an instrument. We model through our behavior what it is we really believe. Parents need to understand this important concept in rearing and training their children.

We direct life through detailed descriptions of what we expect. We do it at home, at work, and in the community. However, we are beginning to realize that small components are not the elements that really effect behavior. Learning theorists Robert Travers and C. Stanislavski suggest that very little evidence exists to support the component approach to teaching. Rather, the evidence indicates that the vital elements of teaching and learning lie at the other end of the behavioral spectrum—in broad characteristics of behavior that form backdrops for creative and productive problem solving. These broad characteristics of behavior are what social psychologists call "mental models."

Stanislavski identifies the need for what he calls "super objectives" to influence the development of mental models. These super objectives are the overriding values that direct behavior. A person who does not have super objectives (or values) can manifest only a patchwork of unrelated skills and disjointed activities. Super objectives give coherence and meaning to the development of our mental models, therefore our behavior.

Simply put, it isn't *what we say* that makes the difference; it's *what we do* that ultimately makes the difference. Mental models shape our perceptions. And if perceptions are the ascribing of significance to experiences, then the heart of the teaching and learning process has to do with filling the "empty self" with appropriate values to guide *what we do.*

We do this through the thoughts we think. As a result, it is necessary for us to enter into a process of thinking about what we value and asking ourselves *who we are* and looking through the window of *who we see ourselves becoming.*

It's important for us to come to understand the mental models that direct our behavior. It is also important that we think about what we model for others—especially our children or students—through our behavior. Is there a difference between *what we say* and *what we do?*

In order to reconcile any dissonance between *who we are* and *what we do*, we have to enter into a process of introspective thought. Some do it through meditation, while others do it through daydreaming, diary keeping, or conversation with those closest to them. Whatever introspective method we choose, it enables us to look into Mirrors before we venture into the dynamics of learning that needs to take place in order to see through the Windows of *who we see ourselves becoming.*

❖ ❖ ❖

At four years of age, Debra's whole life was ahead of her. She was bright and beautiful, with a buoyant, happy personality. The world could be hers, if only . . . "If only." Ever notice how those two words can take the "happily ever after" out of almost any potential fairy tale? In Debra's case, the "if only" has to do with circumstances completely beyond her control. She lives in the housing developments of Chicago, the youngest of four children born to a struggling single mother. Her two older brothers dropped out of school, and her mother never knows whether they are in jail or out. When Debra was three years old her fifteen-year-old sister, herself a new single mother, was killed in a gang fight.

More than anything else in the world, Debra's mother wanted life to be different for her youngest child. So even though she was on welfare and had no education or employable skills to speak of, she worked hard to scrape together enough money to enroll Debra in a pre-school program, hoping that a good pre-school experience would get her daughter's educational career off to a better start than her other children.

"I don't want Debra pregnant at fourteen and dead at fifteen, like her sister," Debra's mother told the pre-school teacher. "I don't want her to have a life like mine. I want her to *be something.* I want her to *be somebody.*"

"I know just what you're saying," the teacher said. Indeed she did. She had grown up just two blocks from where Debra's mother lived. She had come from a similar background and environment. But her mother had done for her just what Debra's mother was doing for Debra, and education became the medium through which she escaped the poverty cycle.

"It isn't easy," the teacher warned. "Debra's going to run into a lot of people in the neighborhood who are going to tell her she's wasting her time on all that schooling. She's going to look around her little world and be hard-pressed to find anyone who has accomplished anything educationally. And she's going to want to quit. I know I did.

"That's when you're going to have to be tough, just like my mother was," the teacher continued. "Your faith is going to have to be strong enough to carry both of you once in a while. You're going to have to teach Debra how to believe in herself by believing in her yourself. You're going to have to help her find models that she can follow, people who have been where she is and have improved themselves."

"You mean people like you?" Debra's mother asked.

"Yes, I guess I do," the teacher replied, hesitantly. "I'm not saying I'm any better than anyone else. But Debra needs to be able to look at people she knows and realize that it can be done."

Debra's mother indicated her willingness to accept her sizeable share of the responsibility the teacher was outlining.

"What we're talking about here is learning," the teacher concluded. "Not just learning the information and skills that school is intended to provide, but learning a whole new way of thinking about the world and Debra's place in it. My philosophy and the philosophy of this school is that we can change our conditions by changing our attitudes. As Debra enters this school, our expectation is that she will succeed."

As this is written, Debra is twelve years old—and she is succeeding. She is doing well in school. She is avoiding the pitfalls that ensnared her brothers and sister. Although she is surrounded by expectations of despair, bitterness, cynicism, and criticism, she has learned to tune out those external influences and stay focused on the vision of life she has created for herself—with help from her mother and some extraordinarily committed teachers.

Clearly Debra has been well-schooled in the focusing power of learning. Although she has not grown up in what most of us would consider an "ideal" home or neighborhood, she has had significant positive support from a mother from whom she has modeled important lessons of commitment and determination. And she has learned that one can rise above one's circumstances to accomplish wonderful things provided one is willing to dream the dream and then work to achieve it. As a result of what she has learned, Debra may one day discover that she is ultimately better off because of the challenges she has encountered (and worked to overcome) than she likely would have been had she been born and raised in affluence.

Like most children, Debra has doubtless heard the story of "The Little Engine That Could"—you know, the one about the little train that pulls a load over a hill that much larger trains couldn't manage simply because he thought he could, he thought he could, he thought he could? Only for Debra it isn't just a story; it's a way of life. She is accomplishing great things because she and others thought she could, thought she could, thought she could. And as a result, she could, and she did.

The expectations we hold for ourselves and for one another create the climate we find in our homes, schools and businesses. In some homes, the people habitually wake up in the morning, look outside drearily and say: "Just as I thought—another stupid day just like every other stupid day." Others embrace each new day, focusing on the beauty of its opportunity and potential. It's a matter of expectation. Which is a matter of attitude. Which is a way of thinking.

That which we call "attitudes" are a critical part of the process of learning. Attitudes are developed as we sift experience through thought and valuing. Attitudes are created by the expectations modeled by others around us. One of the most important factors in improving achievement levels in schools serving underprivileged communities has been the expectations modeled by teachers and administrators in those schools—in other words, their attitudes. Texts and techniques had far less influence than the attitudes of those who worked at the schools and their expectations of what students could accomplish.

As we move from simply reflecting mirrored images of self into looking through windows of personal growth and understanding, we learn through experience the power of our thoughts. Through our thoughts we learn to create mental models based on our beliefs, attitudes, and values. These elements of thought become the model of the future for ourselves and, collectively, for the institutions with which we have influence. They become our expectations.

Doug was a talented runner who specialized in the 400-meter race. Because he was one of the best athletes on his high school track team, he also competed in a couple of relay races. At one of the most important track meets of the year, the team championship came down to the results of the final event: the 1,600-meter relay. Doug had already run several races, and he was pretty well spent physically. But his team was counting on him to run the final leg of the final race, with the championship at stake. So he took his place on the track—and he waited.

When at last he received the baton for the final 400-meter sprint to the finish line there were three runners from other schools in front of him. He ran as fast as he could, but for the first 200 meters he didn't make up much of the distance. As he approached the final turn his legs were heavy and he was struggling. Then, out of the stands, above all the other shouting, came a voice he recognized as his mother's.

"You can do it, Doug!" she shouted as she ran along the rail toward the finish line. "You can do it!"

Somehow his mother's faith and confident expectation gave him the strength he needed to push himself beyond his own expectations. He passed one runner, then another, finally surging into the lead as he crossed the finish line. As he was carried from the track by his jubilant teammates, he heard a familiar, loving voice.

"I knew you could do it, Doug! I *knew* you could do it!"

Our expectations of others send signals of doubt or faith, control or trust. Expectations become self-fulfilling prophecies of victory or defeat. This is especially true in families, where expectations are taught to children through overt and subtle means. The child then conforms to the level of expectation rather than his or her actual level of ability. The parent, in turn, perceives this performance level as the actual ability level, and it becomes so—for good or ill.

As we consider the potential impact and consequence of implied expectation, it's important to remember that hopes and dreams differ from goals and objectives. Typically, a discussion of goals and objectives precedes the development of hopes and dreams. Hopes and dreams are goals and objectives that have become beliefs. Hopes and dreams are goals and objectives governed by faith. Goals and objectives come from the mind and mouth. Hopes and dreams—our mental models—come from the heart and soul.

Expectations and mental models in the form of hopes and dreams influence our behavior at a spiritual level where our hearts, minds, and bodies come together. Unless goals, objectives, and statements of purpose come together at this level of heart, mind, and body, they are only cognitive thoughts, not focusing values.

Many years ago the great psychologist William James developed his famous "as if" principle. If you want to develop a virtue, James taught, act "as if" you already have it. Your own personal hopes and dreams of yourself can produce a permanent change in behavior.

The same principle applies to the creation of hopes and dreams or mental models in homes, schools, communities, and businesses. Set the expectations "as if" the desired results were already reality, and the attainments will come. Just like they did for Debra.

Let's turn our attention now to the power of stories in teaching and learning the mental models that guide our behavior. Stories are known in the helping professions to be one of the most influential teaching tools. Their use in homes, schools, and business organizations is well established through research.

If we are to make a difference in our lives and the lives of others we must understand how the beliefs we are developing are best learned and transmitted. Messages about the purpose and value of our lives are important in educating people. The way they are framed is crucial, and the process by which they are communicated is just as significant.

Words often assume their greatest impact as symbols rather than as literal representations.

Stories can serve as mental models to help people know and see purpose and value. They are also powerful teaching tools.

The ancient art of storytelling is perhaps the most enduring and time-honored teaching method. Researchers in social psychology and speech communications explain that stories excite the imagination of the listener and create consecutive sets of tension and tension release. The listener is not a passive receiver of information, but is triggered into a state of active thinking. The listener must consider the meaning of the story and try to make sense of it. By this process, the listener is engaged; attention and interest are fostered and learning is facilitated.

Rhetorical devices (such as stories, analogies, and metaphors) are persuasive and effective ways to communicate ideas. They can have a substantial impact on values development, and therefore decision-making. Organizational sociologists Joanne Marten and Melanie Powers have demonstrated the power of stories in fostering beliefs. In one case study they tried a number of different methods in an attempt to convince MBA students of the value of certain business practices. Their findings indicated that stories had the greatest impact.

In his book, *Managing by Storying Around,* David Armstrong offers some additional reasons why storytelling is an effective leadership practice: "It's simple; anyone can tell a story. It's timeless; stories are foolproof. It's universally appealing; everybody, regardless of age, gender, and race, listens to stories. It's fun; stories are enjoyable."

Flannery O'Conner, a great American writer, puts it this way: "A story is a way to say something that can't be said any other way . . . You tell a story because a statement would be inadequate."

Our greatest need, says Victor Frankl, is to find meaning in our lives. The most effective therapy, he suggests, would help clients see their lives as being meaningful. Nothing serves this purpose better than the ability to visualize life as a story. E.G. Chesterton, a noted English writer, wrote: "My first and last philosophy, that which I believe in with unbroken certainty, I learned in the nursery . . . The things I believed most in then, the things I believe most now, are the things called fairy tales."

Perhaps most important, stories reinforce the belief that life makes sense—something we are prone to forget from time to time.

The fact is, morality is cast in our mental models. Morality, says William Kilpatrick in *Why Johnny Can't Tell Right From Wrong*, is not a matter of rule-keeping but of role playing. Morality needs to be set within a storied vision if it is to remain morality. Conceived as rule-keeping or as reforming from wrong-doing, it never works for long. Instead, it withers into something cold and cautious and, all too often, into self-righteousness.

An example of this is found in the New Testament in St. Luke. When Jesus was asked by a lawyer, "Master, what shall I do to inherit eternal life?"

Jesus said to him, "What is written in the law? How readest thou?"

The lawyer answered, "Thou shalt love the Lord thy God with all thy heart and with all thy soul and with all they strength, and with all thy mind; and thy neighbor as thyself.

"And he said unto him, thou hast answered right: this do, and thou shalt live."

"But he, willing to justify himself said unto Jesus, and who is my neighbor?

"And Jesus answering said, A certain man went down from Jerusalem to Jericho, and fell among thieves, which stripped him of his raiment, and wounded him, and departed, leaving him half dead.

"And by chance there came down a certain priest that way: and when he saw him, he passed by on the other side.

"And likewise a Levite, when he was at the place, came and looked on him, and passed by on the other side.

"But a certain Samaritan, as he journeyed, came where he was; and when he saw him, he had compassion on him.

"And went to him, and bound up his wounds, pouring in oil and wine, and set him on his beast, and brought him to an inn, and took care of him.

"And on the morrow when he departed, he took out two pence, and gave them to the host, and said unto him, take care of him; and whatsoever thou spendest more, when I come again, I will repay thee.

"Which now of these three, thinkest thou, was neighbor unto him that fell among thieves?

"And he said, He that shewed mercy on him. Then said Jesus unto him, Go, and do thou likewise" (Luke 10:25-37).

Jesus didn't answer by outlining five steps or ten rules. He answered with a story that created a mental model of the value he was trying to teach. In *The Book of Virtues,* William J. Bennett provides the reader with a wealth of stories and verses on ten virtues that he considers essential in our society. One of the stories is Aesop's "The Fox and the Crow," which illustrates the value of using stories to teach a virtue.

> A coal-black crow once stole a piece of meat. She flew to a tree and held the meat in her beak, preparing to dine. A fox who saw her wanted the meat for himself, so he looked up into the tree and said, "How fair you are, my friend. Your shiny black feathers are far more beautiful than the dove's. Is your voice as sweet as your form is lovely? If so, you must be the queen of birds."

> The crow was so pleased and flattered by his praise that she opened her mouth to show how she well could sing. In so doing, the meat fell out of her mouth and down to the ground, where the hungry fox seized upon it and ran away.

According to Bennett, this is a timeless story to teach the virtue of self-control.

Throughout this book we have attempted to capitalize on the power of stories to illustrate and to teach. Some of these stories have come down to us from the past. Others are personal stories that reflect my own background and experience or the experiences of others. Regardless of the source, there is an undeniable link between vision, virtue, and stories. Many people attribute great growth and improvement to being able to see things for the first time or in a different light through stories.

The mental models we create through stories contribute to our goal of controlling consciousness. The "other-directed empty self" can be led through virtuous stories into a process of becoming. Such stories provide vicarious experience, which is sifted through the filters of the mind by thought and enters into a process of valuing. This process of valuing through experience is known as perception, which drives behavior.

Chapter Seven:

Self-Mastery

If one advances confidently in the direction of his dreams, and endeavors to live the life which he had imagined, he will meet with success unexpected in common hours.

—Henry David Thoreau

Sheridan and Celia were enjoying lunch together, and the conversation drifted toward Gordon and Evelyn, a couple familiar to both women.

"You never see Gordon doing anything that you wouldn't expect him to do," Sheridan observed. "He is so consistent, so dependable. I'm sure when he looks in the mirror he's comfortable with what he sees."

"And Evelyn is the same way," Celia agreed. "Neither of them ever seems stressed, regardless of the situation. They just take their time and make their decisions based on what they believe is right for them. I really admire that."

In fact, most of what Celia and Sheridan admired in their neighbors came from Gordon and Evelyn's commitment to the internal values that guided their behavior. It was obvious to them that this couple made choices for living based upon how they felt and what they believed, as opposed to many of us who make choices based upon expediencies and circumstance. Such behavior, they concluded, was characterized by a deep level of commitment to values and visions—or in other words, self-mastery.

For years I have studied and observed people like Gordon and Evelyn to learn what it is that makes them so special. I've compiled these statements that are generally true of such people:

- They don't feel pressured to resolve every issue immediately.
- They accept themselves and others for who and what they are, imperfections notwithstanding.
- They see themselves as significant within themselves, but also part of a greater whole.
- They accept external changes readily because they aren't threatened by them.
- They are optimistic.
- They tend to be active and involved.
- They relate and get along well with others because they sincerely care about others and view them as being important.
- They don't waste time because each day has meaning.
- They are oriented toward a strong set of central core values.
- They are concerned about the welfare of others, including people they've never met and don't know.
- They have learned that real happiness only comes when you step beyond yourself and reach out to others in a meaningful way.
- They have learned that the fastest way to change the world is to change individuals and the way they live their lives.
- They believe that individuality begins with personal honesty about who we are and what we want to be.

That's quite a list, isn't it? But I think we can boil it all down to three manifestations of one essential concept—love. First is love of self, which isn't narcissistic or selfish, but rather, a sincere appreciation for one's own individuality and uniqueness. Next is love of others, born of sincere caring and concern, in which all are esteemed equally. And finally, there is love of God, or something greater than self, which is where our hopes, dreams, and visions of the future rest.

Love is one of the most important concepts of self-mastery we must learn and live. We learn to love in the Mirrors stage by learning to love ourselves. As we become more confident and secure in that love, we can then begin to reach out through Windows of growth and understanding to others, including God.

"If anyone, therefore, will not learn . . . to love himself in the right way, then neither can he love his neighbor," wrote philosopher Sören Kierkegaard. "To love one's self in the right way and to love one's neighbor are absolutely analogous concepts, and at the bottom are one and the same."

Remember John, the Sunday School teacher whose weekday actions were inconsistent with his Sunday instruction? As you recall, Bill, a neighbor, challenged John because there seemed to be significant distance between what he said and what he did.

Thankfully, John's story doesn't end with Bill's challenge. Indeed, that was only the beginning of an important journey for John. It took some time and it was painful, but John eventually learned to bring *who he was* and *what he did* into harmony by focusing his attention more on people than profits. He began talking *with* his employees, not just *at* them. When a sales person had a bad month he looked for *causes,* not just *behaviors.* Slowly, a feeling of real caring enveloped his entire organization. For the first time in his business career John found that his business could be successful without expending a lot of energy motivating sales people with a lot of external tricks and gimmicks.

About two years after their first confrontation at church, John stopped by to visit with Bill.

"Bill," he said, "do you remember that time you asked me if I was the person who taught those wonderful lessons on Sunday or the person who took advantage of you and everyone else during the rest of the week?"

Bill remembered. And he couldn't help but wonder why John was bringing it up again.

"Well," John continued, "I just wanted to thank you for your honesty with me. Your question started a quest in my life that has brought me a lot of happiness and peace."

Bill was pleased—and relieved. "I'm glad it helped," he said. "And I'm interested. What have you learned in your quest?"

"I guess the main thing I've learned is how great it is to have friends and associates who trust you and like you," he said. "I never really had that before, because I guess nobody trusted me. Not that I ever gave anyone any reason to. But now I'm learning to focus on other people and causes in a more positive way. I'm doing things because I think they're the right thing to do, not necessarily because I think they will benefit me or my company in some way."

Bill was curious. "And how has this new philosophy impacted your business?" he asked.

"In terms of sales, it hasn't—not really," John said. "But I feel better about my work and my association with my employees than I ever have before. I'm happier, and I sense that my employees are too."

Thanks in large part to Bill, John has discovered the long-term rewards of happiness and peace that come from a life focused beyond the borders of itself. "To find happiness," wrote W. Bevan Wolfe, a prominent psychiatrist and author, "we must seek for it in a focus outside ourselves."

According to educational psychologist Robert Travers, the mark of mature people is that their living is integrated around self-chosen goals, not imposed goals by the institution or the organization, and not letting circumstances control them. We control circumstances. By expanding self-mastery in our lives we expand our sphere of influence.

We've all found ourselves trapped in situations where we felt we were victimized by circumstances "beyond our control." It's a frustrating, aggravating spot to be in, isn't it? But if we're really honest with ourselves, we have to acknowledge that sometimes those circumstances are only "beyond our control" because we allow them to be. When we place more value in external influences like popularity or the accumulation of money, we are more likely to have a narrow view of the circumstances and situations of our lives—as well as their potential solutions.

"What I must do is all that concerns me, not what the people think," said Emerson in his *Essay on Self-Reliance.* "This rule, equally arduous in actual and in intellectual life may serve for the whole distinction between greatness and meanness. It is the harder because you will always find those who think they know what is your duty better than you know it. It is easy in the world to live after the world's opinion."

Through self-mastery initiated in the Windows stage of life we break away from many of our past external influences and enter a new, broader process of becoming. *Who I think I can become* becomes a dominant way of thinking. Our vision, hopes, and dreams for the future prompt us to learn through study and interaction our place in the world from a variety of different perspectives.

One thing that changes dramatically in the Windows stage is our relationship with others. As we begin to realize greater self-mastery in our lives, we begin to perceive our influence—and potential for influence—upon others. Instead of always thinking about self, we begin to think about how our actions effect others—not for any selfish reasons or motivations, but simply because we've learned to care. Windows relationships begin to build on foundations of trust, understanding, and shared dreams, goals, and visions.

Phil and Barbie had been married for thirteen years. They had two children. Phil was a successful attorney; Barbie had an interior design business that was very time consuming. Both of them were pleasant, articulate, and dynamic. They had a beautiful home, a good family, and considerable social standing in the community. On a strictly superficial level, it appeared that they had everything.

But they didn't. Personal relationships in the family were a shambles. With all of the their various schedules and commitments, there was very little time for meaningful interaction between family members. When they did speak to each other, it was generally to perform some kind of household maintenance or coordination: who is going where when, who is doing what, which car will be available for which activity, and so forth.

It didn't take long in this kind of emotional climate for Phil and Barbie to start drifting away from each other. As they became more distant, they grew less loving toward each other. Their conversations became shorter and more terse. Anger replaced consideration, and arguments became increasingly violent. Eventually they reached the point in their relationship where they went out of their way to aggravate each other. For example, there was the time Phil couldn't find his car keys the morning of an important trial. He was running late anyway, and the missing keys sent him into a fit of frustration. With Barbie gone to work and no cab or bus service in his neighborhood, he had to run the three miles to the court house—a fact made all the more infuriating when Barbie smugly informed him that she had hidden his keys as a way of getting back at him for some hurtful comment he had made the previous evening.

One evening Phil and Barbie found themselves, for the first time in who knows how long, home alone together. For a long time they sat silently, reading the paper, and working on individual projects, but not talking. Finally, Barbie stood and angrily threw her paper to the floor.

"I can't take this anymore!" she said tearfully. "This is ridiculous! Either we need to go our separate ways, or we've got to do something about this hypocrisy we live in. We smile at people we see in public and we act like the perfect family at church. But then we come home and go back into this hateful, morbid personal life we live."

"If you want to leave, go ahead and leave," Phil said quietly. "I'm not going to put the children through a divorce. They've been hurt enough already, laying up in their rooms and listening to us fight."

They sat silently for a few more minutes.

"OK," Barbie said at last, "I'm not leaving, either. But if neither of us is leaving, then we need to find a way to live together peacefully, because I don't think it does anybody any good for us to stay together and live like this."

They agreed to seek professional help, which led them to a broader perspective of the situations and circumstances with which they were wrestling. It was a long and difficult process, but eventually they stopped trying to blame each other and their circumstances for the problems they were having. They realized that their future together rested with each one of them individually. They had to break away from the controls of other people and circumstances. They had to stop looking at past failings as a way to control today's behaviors. They had to restructure their concept of what they were valuing. In so doing, they began to look at themselves and at others in an expanded way.

During the course of this process, their professional activities and priorities began to change. They decided that if they were going to survive as a family they each had to be more in control of their individual destinies. They began to ask themselves what was most important to them and how they could alter the demands upon them and their time so they could focus more attention on the things that really mattered. They reduced their quick-fix responses to immediate problems and introduced more decisions that were the result of study and contemplation.

As they began to take control of their lives and assume more responsibility for their relationships with the other people with whom they lived, they each began to be more responsive to the needs of their colleagues and work associates. Phil, for example, became aware of the struggles of a young associate in the law firm where he worked. He shared his concern for his colleague with Barbie, who suggested that they invite the young man and his family over for a Saturday afternoon barbecue. After lunch and while the children played, Phil and Barbie asked the young couple what they could do to help.

Their young friends were shocked. "We didn't think anyone noticed—or cared," the man said. "We came out of law school with very little money and a lot of debt. And now we've got some medical bills that are creating some real problems for us."

For an hour or more the young couple unloaded their concerns. Phil and Barbie counseled with them as well as they could, and suggested some possible solutions. By the end of the afternoon a warm feeling of friendship permeated the entire group.

"How can we thank you for all that you've done?" the young woman asked as her family prepared to leave.

"You don't need to thank us," Phil said sincerely. "The way I see it, we're all in it together in this world, and anything we can do to help each other . . . well, we just need to do it. Barbie and I have been through tough times, too, and we're grateful for the people who helped us. We all just have to look out for each other."

Five years after he and Barbie started working to rebuild their life together, Phil was invited to meet with the senior partner in his law firm.

"When we hired you," the senior partner said, "we knew you had the potential to be one of the best attorneys in our firm. But to be honest, it took a while for that potential to come through. In fact, we were beginning to lose patience with you and had decided that maybe it was time we both went in different directions.

"Then, about five years ago, something happened," Phil's boss continued. "I don't know what it was, but you started to change. Not just as an attorney, but as a person. You really seem to care about other people, both within our organization and without. And that attitude is contagious. You have had considerable impact on the morale of this entire firm. We know how you have reached out to help your colleagues and associates, and I just wanted to thank you for that. Our office is a better place because you're here. And now we hope you'll be here for many years to come."

Phil wasn't given a partnership that day. He wasn't even given a raise. But as far as he was concerned, he had received one of the greatest rewards of his life. The effort he and Barbie had made to create something significant with their lives based on their values, hopes, and dreams was beginning to have an impact on others, as well. Through self-mastery they were expanding their sphere of influence. With new insight and understanding of themselves, they could now share their dreams and visions with others. No longer were they prisoners of external influences. Rather, they were becoming free citizens of a world where truth and value exist, worthwhile for their own sakes.

Now, before we close this discussion of Windows-based living, I'd like to introduce you to my grandson, Mark. As Mark has grown and matured, one remarkable characteristic of his personality has become evident. He is absolutely unable to intentionally do anything that would harm or injure another person. It's just not in his make-up. And when he injures someone accidentally, he reacts as if he had done the harm to himself. He anguishes over the least unintentional slight. He worries about perceived injustice, no matter who causes it. And when he steps on someone else's toes, he feels their pain.

Such sensitivity to others in one so young is rare, and to tell you the truth, Mark's parents have worried about it a little. They wonder if he's tough enough to deal with the harsh realities of a troubled world. They worry that he has become so giving, unselfish, and loving that unscrupulous others will take advantage of him.

Perhaps they will. But when Mark's parents consider the alternative perspectives available to their son, they are grateful that he is the way that he is. As they observe troubled young people around the world, they recognize that it isn't those who look at the world through positive, helpful eyes of love who have the most serious problems. Rather, those difficulties tend to belong to those whose positive vision is obscured by omnipresent negativity. While Mark's trusting nature may expose him to some hurt along the way, they are wounds from which he will recover. Unfortunately, the same thing cannot always be said of those who lack self-mastery and who view life with cynicism, pessimism, and dread.

Randy certainly encountered more than his share of negativity during his growing up years. And with what some might consider good reason. You see, Randy was born with mental disabilities. Although the exact nature of his problem was never fully explained, doctors and a host of specialists told Randy's parents that he would need special consideration in his schooling. When they refused to consider that counsel, they were warned not to expect too much from their son.

"He'll never be able to function independently in society," they were told. "It will be like having a pre-schooler in your home for the rest of his life."

"That's OK if it works out that way," Randy's mother told her husband. "I like pre-schoolers."

But deep inside both of Randy's parents believed that their son was capable of much more than that. So with extraordinary patience and love they worked to help Randy to achieve his potential—whatever that was. When he was of school age they provided special help to supplement his regular schooling. They pled with neighborhood children to be patient and understanding in their play with him, and three boys actually caught the vision and enjoyed being Randy's friends. While some of the children—and, sadly, adults—made fun of Randy, he never seemed to notice. But he paid careful attention to those who believed in him—his family and a few loyal friends. They told him that he could do anything—and he believed them.

When he was a freshman in high school he joined the track team and became a decent distance runner. He wasn't a star athlete. But that was OK, because Randy didn't want to be a star. He just wanted to be on the team. And he was.

At nineteen, Randy stood before his church congregation and delivered a simple, beautiful sermon about love and acceptance. He spoke clearly, in complete sentences, and he read from his Bible. His family and friends wept as they considered the miracle God had worked in his life through them. And now Randy spoke freely of reaching out to others and blessing them as he had been blessed.

Both Randy and Mark have learned to love themselves, others, and their God by looking through the crystal clear windows of their own pure souls. Through those windows they can see people, causes, truths, and values that are worthwhile for their own sakes. While they have both been influenced to a great degree by others, they are no longer controlled by outside influences. Rather, they are motivated from within by a growing degree of self-mastery over their personal beliefs and values.

The same can be true for all of us. If we focus our attention on bringing *who we are* and *what we do* into harmony through greater self-mastery, we will find ourselves drawing ever closer to authenticity. But we must always remember that it is a process, not a single event. It is through this process that we learn to choose the thoughts and insights that will help us make conscious decisions based on our own dreams, goals, visions, and values.

With our hopes and ambitions firmly in mind, we are now prepared to begin stepping through the doors of opportunity that are open to all those with a sense of vision and destiny. In the Mirrors stage we focused most of our attention on the past and its impact on our lives. In the Windows stage, the future dominated our thinking. And well it should, for it is necessary for us to see through windows to a vision of what we can become. But if we allow ourselves to remain in the Windows stage too long, we may find ourselves continually dreaming of becoming and never really getting down to the important business of doing what needs to be done to become what we are capable of becoming.

So, it is time to move on to the next stage in the process of becoming an *authentic* person. We have taken a look at the various mirrors of self, which have helped us form an image of *who we are* and *who we think we can become.* We have peered with both eyes through windows of growth and understanding, which have helped us to bring *who we are* and *what we do* into greater harmony. Now we must step through the open doors of opportunity—and *become.*

Part Three:

Open Doors
to Timeless Virtues

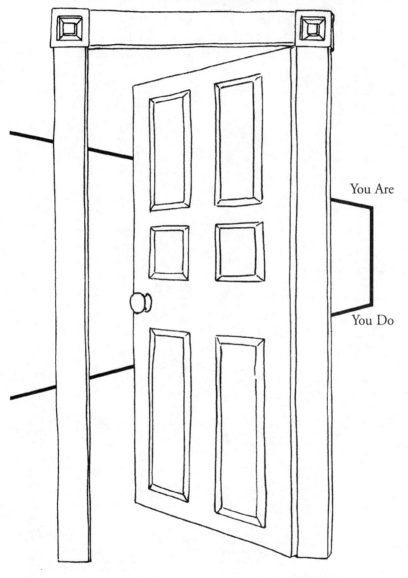

You Are

You Do

OPEN DOORS:
Who I Am

Introduction to Open Doors

Doors are interesting, they open, they close. And the doors we open and close each day decide the lives we live.

—Flora Whittlemore

As we begin to discuss the Open Doors stage, we find ourselves asking "Can we really behave this way in this world as it is? Isn't it too altruistic to think that we can be so different from the world's expectations?"

This type of response has been common. Even my friends and family have questioned the reality of this belief. One of the couples that has been enthusiastic and supportive of my efforts challenged my thinking about entering through the Open Door of service, to truth, gratitude, charity, self-discipline, and courage. I tried to answer the challenge, but upon thinking about it that evening, I chose to sit down and write a letter clarifying my feelings. The following is a copy of my letter to Darrell and Joanne expressing those feelings.

Dear Darrell and Joanne,

For the past couple of months we've been talking off and on about my philosophy of living and growing through Mirrors, Windows, and Open Doors. Our discussions have been detailed— far deeper than the kinds of conversations normally encountered among friends. I am grateful for a relationship like ours that allows time and space for exploration and introspection.

I was particularly impressed with some of the comments Joanne made a few days ago. Remember? You said, "I can understand what you're saying about the Mirrors stage, because I'm experiencing it now and have experienced it in the past. And I think I have a vision of my potential through what you call the Windows stage. But I'm struggling with the concept of Open Doors living. It sounds so unattainable. I mean, are there really people who achieve this level of personal completeness?"

I tried to answer your question the other day, but I don't think I did a very good job of it. So I'm writing this letter in an attempt to respond to your concerns in a more complete and thorough way.

Yes, I do believe Open Doors living can be attained. And if you doubt that, I'd like you to meet a dear friend of mine. Her name is Dorothy.

I met Dorothy thirty-one years ago. At that point in her life she was in what I now call the Mirrors stage, asking herself *who am I?* But she was diligently trying to grow and develop into the Windows stage. She was successfully leaving behind a lifestyle that had filled her life with poverty, cynicism, and sarcasm. She knew the heartaches of divorce and of losing a son to drugs and a life of crime. She knew the struggle of breaking habits that she wanted to leave behind. Her search for peace led her to God, and I watched her in this process of spiritual refinement.

Without knowing it, Dorothy has modeled for me and for many others the process of growth from Mirrors living to Windows living. And now she is proof positive that an Open Doors life is attainable.

Not that such a life is easily maintained. Even today, at this stage of her life, Dorothy deals with adversity. She is on dialysis three times per week, having been near death several times due to diabetes and kidney failure, complicated by a weak heart. I have been by her hospital bed as she recovered from an airplane crash that took the life of her second husband and nearly took her life. Through all of this, I have never heard her convene a "pity party." Every visit with this wonderful woman lifts me and makes me want to try harder. She is my inspiration and my model of what it means to live an Open Doors life.

Yes, Darrell and Joanne, there are real people who have achieved the Open Doors stage. And I truly believe that you and I can reach that goal, too, if we want it and work as hard at it as Dorothy has—life's trials and tribulations notwithstanding.

What it comes down to, I think, is the realization that real happiness only comes when we stop trying to find ourselves in reflected images of others and look instead through the windows of growth to our own personal values and beliefs.

But once we have become secure in ourselves—both in terms of *who we are* and *who we see ourselves becoming*—we can begin to re-evaluate how we relate to other people, places, and situations. As we journey toward becoming *authentic* people, however, we must consider external influences from a position of strength. Confident and self-assured as a result of the growth we have experienced, we can step boldly through the world's open doors, reaching out toward others with kindness, generosity, openness, honesty, understanding, and sincere feeling—not because of external pressures exerted upon us or self-satisfying ulterior motives, but simply because that is the way we choose to live our lives.

One of Dorothy's favorite books is John Steinbeck's *Cannery Row.* I have often heard her recite a significant observation made by Doc, one of the book's characters: "It has always seemed strange to me the things we admire in men—kindness and generosity, openness and honesty, understanding and feeling—are the concomitants of failure in our system. And the traits we detest—sharpness, greed, inquisitiveness, meanness, egotism, and self-interest—are the traits of success. And while men admire the quality of the first, they love the produce of the second."

Doc's statement illuminates the internal tug-of-war most of us experience between our core of virtues and the engine that drives the society in which we live. The desire to be liked and to accumulate more possessions or titles continually contends with the things we claim to value. For example, we say we value honesty and integrity; so what do we do when the boss, whom we know to be highly sensitive, suggests an outrageous and unethical solution to a difficult problem at work? We say we value loyalty and fidelity; so how do we respond to a not-so-subtle come-on from our spouse's attractive colleague? We say we value compassion; so how do we react to the dirty, elderly vagrant we see lying in the street?

As old Zarathustra said, "[we] must not value as [our] neighbor." We must value from within.

As we enter the Open Doors stage we quickly learn that life is a series of interactions between ourselves and others. We also observe the interactions of others. Through our experiences and observations we learn to value. However, it is up to us whether we choose to value according to the world's standards and priorities or our own.

What you will discover, Darrell and Joanne, is that in the Open Doors stage of living we do what we choose to do because we feel the desire to do so from within our inner core of virtues. While we are mindful of past experiences and our dreams for the future, our focus is on the present and living each day to its fullest. We realize that today is the day to fulfill yesterday's dreams, and to build a solid foundation for our vision of tomorrow. As Kalidasa has written:

> For yesterday is but a dream
> And tomorrow is only a vision.
> But today well-lived makes every
> Yesterday a dream of happiness
> And tomorrow a vision of hope.
> Look well, therefore, to this day!

Life offers us two great gifts: time, and the freedom to choose from within the context of our virtues how we will use it. The result of this important interaction—time and choices—produces the consequences of our life. While we are influenced to some degree by external forces and circumstances, it is always up to us to determine for ourselves how we will respond to those forces and circumstances.

If we are to move fully and successfully into the Open Doors stage of our journey toward becoming *authentic* people, our virtues must be more than just another commitment in our busy, frantic lives. They must be forged of sterner stuff, engraved on our hearts and souls, and protected by covenant. For our purposes, let us define "covenants" as solemn agreements we make with ourselves to stay true to our virtues, goals, and beliefs. These are the things that give meaning and purpose to our lives. These are the things we stand for. These are the things we would be willing to die for.

One of Dorothy's favorite movies is *The Wind and the Lion.* In it, Sean Connery plays an Arabic chieftain whose beliefs and values lead him into battle against overwhelming odds. Ultimately, he knows he cannot win. Still, he ventures forth, doing the best he can at what he knows he must do. In the final scene of the film, he and a compatriot are riding their horses along a Mediterranean shore after a narrow escape, a spectacular sunset shimmering metaphorically in the background.

"We have lost everything," his friend moans. "All is drifting on the wind. We have lost *everything*."

Connery's character smiles wistfully and responds: "Is there not one thing in your life that was worth losing everything for?" That statement exemplifies the covenants by which Dorothy has chosen to live. She has found—and she models—what she truly believes. That is an Open Doors approach to living, where success is defined not in terms of accomplishment, but in terms of virtues; where doing the expedient thing isn't as important as doing the right thing; where the only truth that really matters is that you are true to yourself. And that kind of truth, powerful and life-altering, can only be born in the hearts of individuals who have made covenants to honor virtues, goals, and beliefs.

Darrell and Joanne, as we stand on the threshold of Open Doors, it becomes clear to us that we are about to take the most difficult step of all: the last step toward becoming our own person. No longer can we blame other people or external forces and circumstances for our problems. When we become our own person, we accept full responsibility for our decisions and choices. We also accept the consequences of our decisions (although, to be perfectly candid, consequences carry less weight when our decisions are based on our values and beliefs; we do what we do because we think it is right, not because we are trying to achieve—or avoid—some result).

During these past thirty-one years I have watched Dorothy gain greater control over her inner consciousness. Her thoughts have come under her control based on a core of inner virtues she has developed. As you and I mature, we will gain, as Dorothy has, more trust in the processes going on within us. And as we dare to feel our own feelings, we will live by virtues that we discover within.

As fully functioning people, we will find that creative living will emerge. As we progress in the Open Doors stage, we will find more sensitivity and openness to our world. We will become open to all experience—sensitive to what is going on in our environment; sensitive to other individuals with whom we are in relationship; and sensitive, perhaps most of all, to the feelings, reactions, and emergent meanings that we discover within ourselves.

The pull of the "other-directed empty self" will fade. In its place, our focus will change from things, titles, and worldly honors to unity and service with and for others. The "empty self" will be filled with self-chosen intrinsic virtues. The process of valuing will clearly unite in vision and virtue.

We will then see the world with both eyes and with deep perception and clear vision. And in the Open Doors stage of life, we add another dimension as we attain what author-educator Parker Palmer calls "whole sight." We add to our physical view of the world of fact and reason the things one can only see with the heart: a world warmed and transformed by the power of love, a vision of community beyond the mind's capacity to see.

As we unite our mind's eye and our soul, we will develop a unity of *who we are* and *what we do* with others in the world. This unity of *who we are* and *what we do* will develop relationships of trust within our being and in our relationships with others. Peace, serenity, love and service become the hallmark of our living. And please keep in mind, dear friends, that I am describing Dorothy—a living, breathing, vibrant person—with this statement. This is not some obtuse scholar's view of life as it ought to be.

But this harmony of self and others is not complete until the uniting of the soul with faith has taken place in our lives. In his significant book on "optimal experience," Csikszentmihalyl says that "when people try to achieve happiness on their own, without the support of faith, they usually seek to maximize pleasures that are either biologically programmed or are made attractive by the society in which they live."

And if you are uncertain about the concept of the "soul," you're not alone. In *Leading With the Soul*, George Borman and Terry Deal acknowledge that "the word [soul] often sounds strange to modern ears. Terms like 'heart' and 'spirit' seem almost as exotic. We rarely think or talk about where we came from or what we are here to do. We need to; otherwise, we deaden our souls, stunt our spirits, and live our lives half-heartedly." To recapture spirit, we need to re-learn how to lead with the soul, "how to invigorate the family as a sanctuary where people can grow, develop, and find love. How to reinforce the work place with vigor and elan. Leading with soul returns us to ancient spiritual basics—reclaiming the enduring human capacity that gives our lives passion and purpose." What has escaped us is a deep understanding of the spirit, purpose, and meaning of the human experience. I cite this because heart, soul, and spirit are the beacons of Dorothy's life. We need to watch, listen, and learn these virtues.

In the Open Doors stage, Dorothy exemplifies a state of living that is whole-sighted and therefore whole-hearted. Her happy harmony of self, others and faith teaches us that we can be "in the flow"—in the process of becoming—rather than feeling that we have to arrive at some state of rest. In the Open Doors stage of life we experience the present, and are able to live in our feelings and reactions of the moment. We are not bound by the structure of past learning, but we are able to use the past as a present resource to the opportunities of the present moment. The adjectives that most accurately describe Dorothy's life are "enriching," "exciting," "rewarding," "challenging," "meaningful," and "worthwhile." Those same adjectives can describe our lives, if we choose to try.

Of all the virtues Dorothy's life embodies, five seem to me to be absolutely transcendent in our pursuit of authenticity. The first is Truth. And that's just as it should be, because all *authentic* behavior harmonizes in truth. That is what brings together *who we are* and *what we do*. Without a commitment to truth, our behavior can be fuzzy in its focus. Truth brings with it trust, loyalty, and honesty. Without a focus on truth as a central virtue, harmony cannot be fully attained.

The second great virtue is Gratitude. This is one of the least talked about, but most powerful virtues to help us create focus in our pursuit of "whole sight." As an attitude of the mind and soul, gratitude nurtures goodness rather than corruption, commendation rather than criticism, and hope rather than doubt. Gratitude helps us to focus on the blessings of life, as opposed to our natural tendency to believe we haven't been given enough. Gratitude and the concept of "enough" are closely connected in our quest for "whole sight."

The third virtue is Charity, the true love exhibited by the soul. This isn't just an "I love you, dear" kind of love, but a depth of feeling achieved only through a soul-searching quest for truth and faith. Charity comes as we begin to grasp a long-view perspective and a reason for living, which accompanies our personal discovery of a power and purpose greater than self. This kind of "whole sight" makes it possible for us to enter into relationships with others that are truly charitable.

Fourth is Self-Discipline. The "other-directed empty self" is characterized by a lack of self-discipline, as evidenced by the statistics of the day. When 40 percent of school-aged children live in single-parent homes, with projections over the next decade moving toward 60 percent, we have a challenge. The nuclear family, with a father and mother on hand to model virtuous living, must be reinstated in our society. If this is to happen, self-discipline and responsibility must be developed to work through the challenges of family relationships. And if crime, drugs, immorality, and dishonesty are to be dealt with in an "empty self" society, people must assume the responsibility of self-discipline.

And finally, the virtue of Courage focuses on our ability to do what needs to be done. The inner-consciousness must be harmonized in order to gain courage. Our faith in ourselves and others create courage. Covenants, based on virtues for which we would be willing to die, create courage. With courage, you are willing to leave the uncommitted stage of life and enter into covenants with yourself, your neighbors, and your God, and thus gain the harmony and focus of "whole sighted" living.

Our decisions in life are based on our values. When the time comes in our lives to make critical decisions, they tend to be based on the things we value most.

In 1847 a large company of pioneers prepared to cross the Mississippi River and head west under the direction of an experienced, capable wagon master and his young assistant.

"We won't make it before winter with this many people and wagons," the wagon master told his assistant the night before the crossing. "We need half as many people, and they need to be carrying half as much in their wagons if we are to make our journey safely."

The assistant considered the significance of the wagon master's words. He was confident that the man knew what he was talking about, but he also knew that it wouldn't be easy to make the necessary reductions or to decide which families would be left behind. So he asked: "How are we going to do that?"

The wagon master didn't even have to think about his reply.

"Tomorrow morning," he said, "I want you to line up the entire company in ten equal rows, with enough space to drive a wagon between each row. When they have assembled, I want you to tell them what I have told you: that we can only go forward with half as many wagons, and that those wagons will have to reduce their loads by half. Tell them to begin reducing their loads immediately, as we will need to get under way quickly. I will drive down the rows and select our company myself."

The next morning the assistant did as he had been told. Soon after the instructions were given, the wagon master made a slow, purposeful trip up and down the rows. He looked into the pile of discarded belongings and then told each family if they were staying or leaving. By noon the company had been selected and was on its way west. Later that evening the assistant finally worked up the courage to ask the wagon master how he had been able to make so many significant decisions so quickly, and without even talking to the families involved.

"I've learned that you can tell a lot about a person by looking at the things they think are important," the wagon master said slowly. "As I rode up and down the rows, I looked at what they were keeping and what they were willing to leave behind. If they thought that china and silver were more important than blankets and seed and medical supplies, then I didn't want them in my company. But if they were able to decide quickly to leave behind the valuables and carry only the essentials, then I figure they're going to be able to come through when the troubles hit. Those are the kind of folks I want to have traveling with me."

The wagon master made his choices by watching others think quickly through their priorities and make choices. With keen insight he understood that their choices reflected their values, and he was able to put together a successful company based on his thoughts and impressions of those reflected values.

Thus it is with each of us. People trust us—or don't trust us—based on their perception of the values our choices represent. And our choices come from our own thoughts about the virtues we have covenanted with ourselves to embrace.

That's the essence of Open Doors living, Darrell and Joanne. It is a life filled with truth, gratitude, charity, self-discipline, and courage, among other virtues. Please keep in mind that these are not simply the philosophical meanderings of an idealistic social scientist. These concepts are real. I have seen them at work in the lives of extraordinary people like Dorothy. Doubtless you have known a Dorothy or two in your lives, as well. The door to authenticity is open (if you'll pardon the expression) to all of us who are prepared to step through. And if you ask me, I think both of you are just about ready to take that step.

Congratulations! And good luck on the rest of your journey!

Chapter Eight:

The Virtue of Truth

Oh, the comfort, the inexpressible comfort of feeling safe with a person, having neither to weigh thoughts nor measure words, but pouring them all out, just as they are, chaff and grain together; certain that a faithful hand will take and sift them, keep what is worth keeping, and then with the breath of kindness blow the rest away.

—Dinah Craik

My friend and colleague, Lloyd, taught me a lot about the virtue of truth. I met Lloyd years ago, when we were both working as educational administrators. He was a veteran, just five years away from retirement; I was a rookie. My first day on the job, Lloyd was the one who volunteered to ride with me on a tour of our schools and facilities.

"I'd love to go with you," he said. "It'll give me a chance to show off my new suit!" And a fine, handsome suit it was. I had already noticed it and expressed my admiration. Now, it seems to me that you can tell a lot about a person's self-esteem by the way they respond to a compliment. People with too much self-confidence will often use the compliment as a way to tell you the whole story behind whatever it is you complimented—where they got it, what wonderful quality it is, how they haggled with the sales clerk to get a better deal, and so forth. Those who lack self-confidence will usually try to tell you that, oh, it isn't really that great, or yours is better, or it wasn't exactly what they wanted, or something like that. Lloyd responded to my compliment of his suit simply, with a warm smile and a sincere "Thank you!" Immediately, he struck me as a man who was at peace with himself.

So we hopped into my car, with me driving and Lloyd navigating. We chatted comfortably for several minutes, enjoying our new acquaintance, until Lloyd told me to pull into . . . *a fast food establishment?!?!*

"This is the first stop on our tour," he announced, matter-of-factly. "Root beers are on me!"

Lloyd, I soon came to understand, was something of a root beer connoisseur. He knew where the best root beer could be purchased for the best price, and he rarely traveled anywhere without a root beer in hand. He even had definite ideas about how a root beer should be sipped.

"Straws dilute the flavor and carbonation," he said. "You've got to sip root beer from an open lid to get the full effect."

Which is why Lloyd and I were driving through town with large, open root beers in our hands when I came to that traffic signal. We had been enjoying our conversation (in between sips of root beer, of course), and I hadn't noticed that the light had turned red. When at last I did notice I was almost into the intersection, and I had to slam on the brakes to stop.

Thankfully, I had sipped enough of my root beer that I was able to control the beverage sloshing around in my cup without spilling any. But Lloyd wasn't so lucky. I hit the brakes just as he was taking a big swig from his cup, and he ended up dumping most of its contents on his suit. His beautiful *new* suit.

I was mortified, and my apologies were profuse. But Lloyd could only laugh—genuinely and absolutely without rancor—at his predicament.

"Hey," he said, "I told you that the root beer was on me, didn't I? Besides, the salesman bragged about how well this suit would clean. Now I'm going to have a chance to see if he was right."

"Well, I'll pay for the cleaning," I insisted.

"Curtis, this is so unimportant," he said, indicating the spilled root beer and the stained suit. "Please don't worry about it." Then his voice turned somber and serious. "But there is one thing you *could* do for me—something *really* important."

"Anything," I said, anxious for a chance to make things right.

"Pull into the next fast food place," Lloyd said. "I need some more root beer!"

That's just the way Lloyd was: calm, patient, generous, kind. You didn't have to be a psychologist to see that Lloyd was comfortable with himself. And because he was comfortable, he made the world around him a more comfortable, peaceable, pleasant place.

I wasn't the only one who noticed. Almost everyone who interacted with Lloyd was influenced by him in a positive way. One day I was working on a project in our basement at home, and had asked my family to take messages from anyone who called me so I could move forward with my work uninterrupted. I was a little perturbed when my son, Douglas, then 4 years old, appeared at the top of the stairs.

"Dad!" he called, "You're wanted on the telephone! Hurry!"

"I thought I told you not to bother me right now!" I spoke with irritation. "Take a number and I'll call back!"

"But it's important, Dad. You *want* to talk to him."

"I do? Who is it?"

"Oh, you know," Doug said. "It's the man who likes me so much!"

"The man who likes me so much!" Yes, that had to be Lloyd, because that's how everyone felt in his presence. Not because he was especially glib, articulate, or flowery—he wasn't. Nor was he the most dynamic person I've ever met. But he did make an impact. He affected lives. People left classes or meetings with him uplifted and enriched because they had spent some time with "the man who likes me so much."

After months of watching Lloyd make a difference in the lives of those with whom he came in contact, I asked him to share his secret with me.

"There's no secret, really," he said. "Like everyone else, life has taught me some important lessons—sometimes the hard way."

When he was still in his twenties, his young wife became ill and died quite suddenly. To that point, he told me, he had taken life for granted. "I didn't have any real purpose or direction," he said. "Most of my decisions were spontaneous, usually based on the expectations of others. Soon after my wife died, it occurred to me that she had never even known me. All she knew was this shallow young man who drifted wherever the winds of fortune blew him. It made me feel sad and unfulfilled.

"But what really haunted me was the realization that I couldn't recover the time that was lost. I mean, here I was, this young man, and already I was beginning to feel that life was passing me by."

With that realization, however, came the subsequent understanding that, as a young man, he had time to make changes in his life. But he knew he had to make a decision immediately.

"Was I going to continue living as I had lived, a slave to outside influences and past experiences," he said, "or was I going to 'seize the day' and make a future for myself out of what seemed, at the moment, a heap of ashes?"

It was a critical moment in Lloyd's life, just as it is for all of us when we reach the crossroads of that most significant decision. All of the wonderful traits and abilities that I saw in Lloyd years later stemmed directly from the decision he made at that critical moment in his life. Aimlessness and hopelessness have been replaced by direction and hope.

Lloyd's quest was to bring into harmony all the parts of life that give it meaning. What a sensitive, wonderful way to be known: "the person who likes me so much."

How does one arrive at a point in life where they can be known in the way Lloyd was known? First, we have to enter into a period of introspection. We have to look into the mirrors of self and create a thought process that will allow us to know the truth about ourselves. Each of us needs to experience this process in our lives.

But introspection alone is not enough. We must also act on the impulses and impressions of our introspection. Joined together, the introspection and the doing produce the beautiful pictures in life that become the mental models of our behavior.

According to Lloyd, truth was the central virtue of his quest.

"But how do you find truth?" I asked him.

His response was succinct: "By being truthful."

Then he told me a story from his past to illustrate the point. "Curtis," he said, "you know that I buy and sell a few horses now and then." I did, and I knew how excited he got when a good deal was in the making.

"Well," he continued, "the other day a friend of mine came by to see if I had a nice, quiet family horse. I didn't, but I told her about this fellow I know out in Lizard Gulch. 'He's got some nice horses,' I told her, 'but you've got to watch out for him. He can be pretty cagey.'"

So she went out to Lizard Gulch and asked the old fellow if he had a nice, quiet family horse to sell.

"I do," he said, "but he don't look too good."

My friend assured the horse trader that she didn't care how the horse looked as long as it was gentle.

"Well, he's gentle, all right," he said. "But I want you to know that this horse don't look too good."

When my friend finally saw the horse, she wondered why the old gentleman found the animal so unattractive. It was a handsome horse, and clearly quiet and docile in its behavior. So the sale was made, and my friend took her new horse home to her family.

After working with the horse for a while, it became clear that the animal was blind. My friend went back to Lizard Gulch and scolded the old fellow for selling her a blind horse.

"I always tell the truth," the old man said indignantly. "I told you the horse didn't look too good."

Lloyd chuckled as he finished telling me the story. "Remember," he said, "the word 'truth' means different things to different people. Sometimes we even deceive ourselves into thinking that we're telling the truth when we really aren't. The way I see it, self-deceit equals self-defeat. That's why I say that the best way to learn truth is to be truly truthful."

William George Jordan, an early Twentieth-Century philosopher from Harvard, defined truth as "the rock foundation of every great character. It is loyalty to the right as we see it; it is courageous living of our lives in harmony with our ideals; it is always—power. Truth ever defies full definition. Like electricity, it can only be explained by noting its manifestations. It is the compass of the soul, the guardian of conscience, the final touchstone of right. Truth is the revelation of the ideal; but it is also an inspiration to realize that ideal, a constant impulse to like it. Truth is the oldest of all virtues. When a great truth is grasped in morals, we have in it the key to spiritual re-creation. Truth is living simply and squarely by our beliefs."

Truth is not just an early Twentieth-Century concept or even a Garden of Eden concept; it is a today concept. In *The Fifth Discipline*, organizational behaviorist Peter Senge begins his discussion of organizational transformation by advocating "a disarmingly simple, yet profound strategy for dealing with structural conflict: telling the truth."

Authenticity is centered in truth. The journey to authenticity is, in fact, a journey to truth. Like all other virtues, truth is less a set of techniques and methods than it is a feeling of the soul. According to Senge, truth is a relentless willingness to root out the ways we limit or deceive ourselves from seeing what is, and to continually challenge our theories of why things are the way they are.

"The power of truth is seeing reality more and more as it is," Senge continues, "cleansing the lens of perceptions, awakening from self-imposed distortions of reality—different expressions of a common principles exist in all the world's great philosophic and religious systems. Buddhists strive to achieve the state of 'pure observation,' of seeing reality directly. Hindus speak of 'witnessing' and observing themselves and their lives with an attitude of spiritual detachment. The Koran ends with the phrase, 'what a tragedy that man must die before he wakes up . . . The truth shall set you free."

Seeking the truth is an integral part of the quest for control of inner consciousness. As we gain a more focused understanding of truth, we can shed the challenges of society's "other-directed empty self" characteristics.

The outgrowth of truth is authenticity or trust, honesty, exactness, uprightness, faithfulness and trustworthiness. The absence of truth means opposite traits are present: falsehood, lying, prevarication, fabrication, falsification, deception, invention, misrepresentation, suppression, exaggeration, evasion and insincerity. Consider those two lists of characteristics. Then look in the mirror and see yourself in light of the virtue of truth.

According to a story in Bennett's *Book of Virtues,* Truth and Falsehood once met each other on the road.

"Good afternoon," said Truth.

"Good afternoon," replied Falsehood. "And how are you doing these days?"

"Not very well at all, I'm afraid," sighed Truth. "The times are tough for a fellow like me, you know."

"Yes, I can see that," said Falsehood, glancing up and down at Truth's ragged clothes. "You look like you haven't had a bite to eat in quite some time."

"To be honest, I haven't," Truth admitted. "No one seems to want to employ me nowadays. Wherever I go, most people ignore me or mock me. It's getting discouraging, I can tell you. I'm beginning to ask myself why I put up with it."

"And why the devil do you? Come with me and I'll show you how to get along. There's no reason in the world why you can't stuff yourself with as much as you want to eat, like me, and dress in the finest clothes, like me. But you must promise not to say a word against me while we're together."

So Truth promised and agreed to go along with Falsehood for a while, not because he liked his company so much, but because he was so hungry he thought he'd faint soon if he didn't get something into his stomach. They walked down the road until they came to a city, and Falsehood at once led the way to the very best table at the very best restaurant.

"Waiter, bring us your choicest meats, your sweetest sweets, your finest wine!" he called, and they ate and drank all afternoon. At last, when they could hold no more, Falsehood began banging his fist on the table and calling for the manager, who came running at once.

"What the devil kind of place is this?" Falsehood snapped. "I gave the waiter a gold piece nearly an hour ago, and he still hasn't brought our change."

The manager summoned the waiter, who said he'd never even seen a penny out of the gentlemen.

"What?" Falsehood shouted, so that everyone in the place turned and looked. "I can't believe this place! Innocent, law-abiding citizens come in to eat, and you rob them of their hard-earned money! You're a pack of thieves and liars! You may have fooled me once, but you'll never see me again! Here!" He threw a gold piece at the manager. "Now this time bring me my change!"

The manager, fearing the restaurant's reputation would suffer, refused to take the gold piece, and instead brought Falsehood change for the first gold piece he claimed to have spent. Then he took the waiter aside and called him a scoundrel, and said he had a mind to fire him. And as much as the waiter protested that he'd never collected a cent from the man, the manager refused to believe him.

"Oh, Truth, where have you hidden yourself?" the waiter wondered. "Have you now deserted even us hard-working souls?"

"No, I'm here," Truth groaned. "But my judgement gave way to my hunger, and now I can't speak up without breaking my promise to Falsehood."

As soon as they were on the street, Falsehood gave a hearty laugh and slapped Truth on the back. "You see how the world works?" he asked. "I managed it all quite well, don't you think?"

But Truth slipped from his side. "I'd rather starve than live as you do," he said.

And so Truth and Falsehood went their separate ways, and never traveled together again.

When we see truth, *who we are* and *what we do* are the same. Having a "whole sight" in life occurs when the mind's eye and the soul are one. When that happens in our lives, we will truly experience truth.

Chapter Nine:

The Virtue of Gratitude

We take for granted the very things that most deserve our gratitude.

—Cynthia Czick

Gratitude is a feeling of the soul. As Samuel Johnson said, Gratitude is a fruit of great cultivation; you do not find it among gross people." It is the instinctive radiation of justice, giving new life and energy to the individual from whom it emanates.

Gratitude is associated with character qualities like peace, serenity, and satisfaction. As a virtue, gratitude creates optimism, not pessimism; hope, not doubt; and confidence, not insecurity. According to the old sailing song, "When our perils are past, shall our gratitude sleep? No, here's to the pilot that weathered the storm."

Gratitude and giving are inseparably connected. Conversely, ingratitude is similarly linked to taking.

During the course of our lives, we have all known givers and takers. It seems to me that the takers are those who have failed to gain the virtue of gratitude. They are never genuinely grateful, therefore they never have "enough."

On the other hand, the givers I have known tend to be grateful for what they have. They are surrounded by an air of peace and serenity. Their happiness seems to come from giving. Gratitude is truly a refinement of character that is found in those who have developed an inner-peace and have found "enough."

"Enough" is an interesting concept, isn't it? In the film *Cool Runnings,* the coach of the Jamaican Olympic bobsled team is seen explaining to one of his team members how he had fallen into the trap of cheating—thus depriving himself and his team of a gold medal—when he was an Olympic bobsledder years earlier.

"Coach," the young bobsledder asks, "why did you cheat?"

"I don't know," the coach says. "I guess I just wanted that gold medal so much that I was willing to do anything to get it."

"But you already had gold medals," the young athlete points out.

"I know," the coach replies. "But somehow it wasn't enough. So I cheated to get another. I never felt I had enough, and it has ruined my life."

The younger bobsledder pauses for a moment, then asks: "Coach, when will I know when I have enough?"

"You'll know," the coach says, "when you feel it within yourself."

Look around, and I'm sure you'll see people in your life who have achieved "enough"—and not because they are fabulously wealthy or the world's greatest . . . whatever. They are content because they are at peace with themselves and the world around them. They find life fulfilling for its own sake, not for what it brings to them or for any station they have achieved. And they are grateful.

My father provided me with a model of this significant virtue. He was a man of humble means, a teacher who loved teaching almost as much as he loved raising Suffolk sheep on the small farm where we lived. On one occasion and at considerable sacrifice he bought an expensive Suffolk buck at the state fair. For several years the buck was bred to my father's little herd of ewes. And then one day my father decided to sell his buck, and he ran an ad in the paper.

The first people who came to see the buck was a family in an old, well-worn car. The man, his wife and their three small children were all excited about the buck. They were sure he was just what they needed to start a fine herd of Suffolk sheep, and they made an offer.

"Unfortunately," the father said, "I don't have that much money right now. But I could pay $5 a month until the whole amount is paid."

The entire family looked at my father hopefully. The next thing I knew, he was easing the buck into the back seat of the family's old car. "You need him more than I do," I heard him say to the man. "If you ever get some extra money, pay me whatever you can."

I was stunned. While I appreciated the gesture, I knew that my father couldn't afford to be so generous. As the happy family drove off, I shook my head and sighed. "I hope you're not really expecting to get anything back from that family," I said, my voice edged with resignation. "They'll never pay you what that old buck is worth."

"Maybe not," my Dad said. "But isn't it great to have all that we have, and to be able to share?"

Even as young as I was, I was impressed by my father's focus on what he had, not on what he didn't have. And somehow, his gratitude made me more grateful, as well.

Gratitude is a virtue of people who are able to see, through a process of valuing goodness in their environment. Because *who they are* and *what they do* are one and the same, they don't feel threatened by external influences. Therefore, they tend to see others as good, and they seek opportunities to serve.

As desirable as this marvelous virtue is, however, I have found much more written on the subject of ingratitude than on the subject of gratitude. The life of Jesus Christ, as summarized by William George Jordan, was a tragedy of ingratitudes, manifest in three phases, or degrees of intensity. The first and most common phase of ingratitude Jordan notes is thoughtless thanklessness. When Jesus healed ten lepers in one day, only one returned to Christ to express gratitude. The other nine departed without a word—thoughtlessly thankless.

The second phase of ingratitude, according to Jordan, is denial—a positive sin, not the mere negation of thanklessness. This was exemplified by Peter, one of the leading disciples of Jesus. While Jesus was being judged and prepared for execution, Peter was confronted and asked if he was a follower of Christ. Because he lacked the courage of his convictions, he forgot his friendship and loyalty to his Master and denied him—not once or twice, but three times.

And finally, Jordan refers to treachery as the third phase of ingratitude. This is when selfishness becomes vindictive, as illustrated by Judas Iscariot, the honored treasurer among the followers of Jesus, whose greed, jealousy, and ingratitude led directly to Christ's ignominious death by crucifixion.

These three phases—thanklessness, denial, and treachery—run the gamut of ingratitude in a sort of domino effect. Thanklessness leads to denial, and denial prepares the way for treachery.

Ralph Smith, head of a large department in his company, read Jordan's insights on gratitude and was impressed by them. He thought they would have application in his company, and so he asked the managers who worked under him to participate in an important learning activity. After teaching the managers about the phases of ingratitude, he asked them to take a look at what was going on in the work place around them.

"What I want you to do," he said, "is to quietly focus your attention on the interactions that take place during a normal day in your area. Make notes of the conversations you have and the activities that take place among those with whom you work.

"At the end of the day," Smith continued, "sit down and summarize interactions and events. Determine how many times not having 'enough' has influenced a behavior. Consider the kinds of behavior that result from an attitude of 'enough'."

The next day Smith met with his managers again to discuss the experience. "It was a little dismaying," Smith said later. "We were pleased to identify people whose behaviors reflected feelings of thankfulness, service, and kindness. These were people who helped and encouraged others and who lifted and built colleagues and the organization. These were people who seemed to feel they had *enough*.

"On the other hand," Smith continued, "we observed many people who felt they were entitled to more. They didn't have *enough*. Their behavior demonstrated thankless thoughtlessness. They were not totally supportive of the goals of the organization. There were also cases of denial because of not having 'enough. And there were even instances of treachery, where the feelings of not having *enough* were so deep that employees were participating in dialogue bordering on rebellion and revolt."

Smith and his managers vigorously discussed the experience at length, often correlating "good people" with gratitude and "bad people" with ingratitude. Finally Paul, a senior supervisor, asked for the floor.

"I've been with this company for twenty-five years," he said. "During that time, I've heard a lot of talk about good and bad attitudes and behavior, but this is the first time anyone has talked to us about the virtue of gratitude and how it influences our behavior. It's been an enlightening experience, but also frightening. And the most frightening thing about it is I find myself questioning my own feelings of gratitude and ingratitude. Have I been a grateful employee and supervisor, or have I been ungrateful? Have I shown my gratitude for my colleagues, or do I communicate ingratitude?

"I'm a little uncomfortable with the answers to those questions," Paul continued. "For the first time in my life I'm looking at the impact of a virtue on my behavior, and quite frankly, I don't like everything I'm seeing and I'm anxious to start making some changes. And that makes me wonder if the same thing can't happen for our employees. What if we start a conversation among our employees about gratitude and its influence on our behavior, instead of focusing all our attention on the behaviors themselves?"

It was an excellent suggestion, one that had real impact on the workers, their supervisors and the company itself.

The following verse by an unknown author illustrates the thoughtless thanklessness that permeates many lives:

Why didn't I remember to say "Good-bye,"
  "I love you" and "Have a happy day today?"
And "Thanks again for trying to be my friend,
  Because I couldn't make it any other way."

But you just don't say those kinds of things to your Dad in the morning.
It's "Pass the salt!" or "I'm late, I've got to go!" that's about all.
Oh, I wish I'd seen a vision or a dream how I'd miss him so when I have to go.
How do I let him know?

I missed my chance to tell him about my romance last summer.
  I didn't think he'd understand.
It never entered my mind, he may have had the very same kinds of feelings when he first held my mother's hand.

But you just don't say those kinds of things to your Dad in the evening.
It's "I've gotta run, everyone is waiting for me, can I use your car?"
  "No, I won't go far."
Well, it wasn't far then, it was just around the bend.
  And now it's ten thousand miles and it's gonna be a while 'till we meet again.

I've tried since then to make my pen convey
  The message that I've neglected all these years.
But the words come slow, and there's so much I want him to know.
  And the time to say "I love you, Dad" is here.

But how do you write those kinds of things to your Dad in a
letter?

Things you never took the time to tell him face-to-face?
But I wrote him, and I learned from a very special letter in return
how much
my Father knew
About what my soul has been going through.
You see, it happened to my Dad, too.

I love you, Dad!

We are all guilty of such ingratitude from time to time: the
spouse who criticizes his or her partner in public or group settings;
the worker who gossips about a colleague; the neighbor who belittles
others in the neighborhood; the church member who incites others
in the congregation against their minister. Thanklessness becomes
denial, which can become treachery. One leads almost inevitably to
another, and we can become blind to the many things for which we
have to be grateful. It's like the farmer who found his son out in the
stable, enthusiastically digging through piles of manure. When his
father asked him how he could possibly be so excited about such an
unpleasant task, the boy looked up at him with a happy smile. "The
way I see it," said the lad, "with all of this manure, there has to be a
pony around here somewhere!"

Gratitude is an attitude we choose. It is the result of looking for
and finding the good in life—despite the bad. Being grateful helps us
maintain a broad perspective in the face of events and situations that
might make our focus more limited and narrow. Reminding ourselves
about what is right with our lives can become a self-fulfilling prophesy.

My friend Lloyd and I remained close for many years. His
influence on my life was significant. After he retired, however, our
time together grew less and less frequent until one day I realized that
it had been five years since I'd seen him. From time to time I'd make
a mental note to myself to pay Lloyd a visit, but something else
always came up. Then one day I received a telephone call informing
me that Lloyd had passed away.

I was sorrowful—and ashamed. If Lloyd had taught me anything it
was that there is no time like the present—right now—to reach out to
others with love and compassion. And yet I had allowed the business
of living to rob me of one last opportunity to be with my old friend.
The words of a poem by Charles Hanson Towne came forcefully to
my mind:

Around the corner I have a friend
In this great city that has no end.
Yet days go by, and weeks rush on
And before I know it a year is gone.
And I never see my old friend's face,
For life is a swift and terrible race.

He knows I like him just as well
As in the days when I rang his bell
And he rang mine. We were younger then,
And now we are busy, tired men:
Tired with trying to make a name.
"Tomorrow," I say, "I will call on Jim
Just to show that I'm thinking of him."
But tomorrow comes—and tomorrow goes,
And the distance between us grows and grows.

Around the corner! Yet miles away.
"Here's a telegram, sir."
"Jim died today."
And that's what we get and deserve in the end.
Around the corner, a vanished friend.

Gratitude is not about gentle thoughts or noble intentions. It's about doing—now, *today.* We must honor, cherish, and value the present moment, for it is the only phase of our existence over which we have control. "The only time that is surely yours is the present," said Grenville Kleiser, "hence, this is the time to speak the word of appreciation and sympathy, to do the generous deed, to forgive the fault of a thoughtless friend, to sacrifice self a little more for others."

Today is the only day to make your life meaningful and worthwhile. Yesterday is gone; tomorrow may never come. The present is all that you have to do with as you will. If we are ever going to bring our beliefs, visions, and values together and harmonize *who we are* and *what we do,* it has to be today. Expressions of gratitude put off until tomorrow have a way of stacking up, losing individual significance in the clutter of procrastinated priorities. Then one day we run out of tomorrows, and it's too late to do anything about all of those empty yesterdays but wonder what might have been had we put today to better use.

In Victor Hugo's classic *Les Miserables,* Jean Valjean is released from prison after nineteen years of harsh and dehumanizing treatment. As he travels home from prison, he is treated like a stray dog until he meets the Bishop of Digne, a man whose life is directed by the peace and serenity of virtuous gratitude. I love the words of greeting the character of the Bishop sings in the musical version of *Les Miserables:*

> Come in, sir, for you are weary and the night is cold out there,
> Though our lives are very humble, what we have we have to share.
> There is wine here to revive you. There is bread to make you strong.
> There's a bed to rest 'til morning. Rest from pain and rest from wrong.

As he rests at the good Bishop's home, Valjean sings his thoughts:

> He let me eat my fill.
> I had the lion's share.
> The silver in my hand
> Cost twice what I had earned
> In all those nineteen years,
> That lifetime of despair.
>
> And yet he trusted me.
> The old fool trusted me.
> He'd done his bit of good.
> I played the grateful serf
> And thanked him like I should.
> But when the house was still
> I got up in the night,
> Took the silver,
> Took my flight!

Jean Valjean leaves, but is caught and brought back to the Bishop. When Jean Valjean tells his captors that the Bishop gave him the silver, the Bishop not only agrees, but suggests to the officers that his guest had left behind other gifts he had given to him. After the officers leave, he offers counsel to the stunned Valjean that transforms the recently released convict:

> Remember this, my brother, see in this some higher plan.
> You must use this precious silver to become an honest man.
> By the witness of the martyrs, by the passion and the blood,
> God has raised you out of darkness. I have bought your soul for God.

Later in the musical production, Jean Valjean recalls this powerful experience with gratitude—gratitude for the plan, gratitude for the Bishop's gift and gratitude for the gift of life:

What have I done?
Sweet Jesus, what have I done?
Become a thief in the night?
Become a dog on the run?
And have I fallen so far,
And is the hour so late
That nothing remains but the cry of my hate?
The cries in the dark that nobody hears.
Here where I stand at the turning of the years.

Yet why did I allow this man
To touch my soul and teach me love?
He treated me like any other.
He gave me his trust.
He called me his brother.
My life he claims for God above.
Can such things be?
For I had come to hate the world,
This world that always hated me.

The greatest gift to Jean Valjean from the Bishop is a mental model of gratitude so powerful that it guides the rest of his life.

In our lives in the Open Door stage, we begin to see with "whole sight" through the lens of gratitude. I have come to believe that the virtue of gratitude precedes many others as a tool of valuing in our lives.

Of course, the major deterrent to the development of gratitude is pride. Pride and gratitude are at enmity, which is defined as "hatred toward, hostility to, or a state of opposition." Pride is essentially competitive in nature, whereas gratitude is cooperative. Those who are proud have a difficult time accepting the authority of others, while those who are truly grateful tend to be humble and tolerant. Proud people elevate themselves above others, even if they have to diminish them to do it; grateful people, not threatened by the accomplishments of others, celebrate the accomplishments of others even if it places others above themselves.

The proud make every one their adversary by pitting their intellects, opinions, works, wealth, talents or any other worldly measuring device against others. C.S. Lewis writes, "Pride gets no pleasure out of having something, only out of having more of it than the next man . . . It is the comparison that makes you proud! The pleasure of being above the rest. Once the element of competition has gone, pride has gone."

The proud compete on all levels of activity in life, pitting their talents, wealth, works, opinions, and intellects or any other worldly measuring device against others. Pride is a totally self-serving, "empty self" condition. Gratitude is the virtue that results from overcoming the self-serving, "I am better than you" nature of pride. Gratitude creates humility, peace, and serenity within that allows the opportunity to reach out to others. Gratitude gives us the opportunity to bring the art of helping others to a higher level.

> Wouldn't this old world be better
> If folks we meet would say,
> "I know something good about you!"
> And then treat us that way!
>
> Wouldn't it be fine and dandy
> If each hand clasp warm and true
> Carried with it this assurance:
> "I know something good about you!"
>
> Wouldn't life be lots more happy
> If the good that's in us all
> Were the only thing about us
> That folks bothered to recall?
>
> Wouldn't life be lots more happy
> If we praised the good we see?
> For there's such a lot of goodness
> In the worst of you and me.
>
> Wouldn't it be great to practice
> That fine way of thinking, too?
> You know something good about me!
> I know something good about you!
>
> —*Author Unknown*

From the "Ode for Music" we read, "Sweet is the breath of vernal shower, the bee's collected treasures sweet, sweet music's melting fall, but sweeter yet, the still small voice of gratitude."

An attitude of gratitude lays a foundation through which we can see with "whole sight" through the eyes of the mind and the soul, and lay the groundwork for the development of the next great virtue we will consider: the virtue of charity.

Chapter Ten:

The Virtue of Charity

The ultimate lesson all of us have to learn is unconditional love, which includes not only others but ourselves as well.

—Elisabeth Kubler-Ross

Have you ever noticed how the meaning of some words changes with time and usage? "Cool" used to be a weather report. "Rap" used to be something you did with your knuckles. And if someone said they were feeling "happy and gay," you weren't inclined to make any assumptions about their sexuality.

The same thing is true of the word "charity." While we tend to think of it as a handout, or an organization for those who are somehow less fortunate, there was a time when it meant something much, much more. One of the writers of the New Testament, St. Paul, said that charity is, along with faith and hope, one of the three greatest traits to which we can aspire. Indeed, Paul said that "the greatest of these is charity" (1 Corinthians 13:13).

"Charity," he said, "never faileth."

You don't have to accept Paul's theology to find wisdom in his philosophy and valuable guidance on your journey toward becoming an *authentic* person. What a wonderful world it would be if we could all become more charitable. Abuse would fade, bigotry would disappear, selfishness would become passé; and joy, peace, and serenity would dominate world affairs and human relationships.

The apocryphal story is told of two orphaned children—an eight-year-old boy and his five-year-old sister, who was critically ill. Compounding the girl's problem was the fact that her blood type was incredibly rare; indeed, her older brother was the only person in the community who shared it. When doctors finally decided that emergency surgery would be required to save the little girl's life, they had no choice but to go to her older brother for precious, life-saving blood. Carefully, they explained as well as they could the girl's dangerous position. They told him that he could be a hero by giving his blood to her.

"Will it hurt?" he asked hesitantly, uncertainly.

"Not much," the doctor replied. "Oh, you'll feel a little discomfort when we put the needle in your arm, but you won't really . . . "

"No," the boy interrupted. "I mean, will it hurt *her?*"

"Oh, no," the doctor said, impressed by the lad's concern for his sister. "She won't feel a thing. Except she'll feel a lot better as soon as we get your blood in her."

The boy thought quietly for a moment. The doctor could see that he was choking back huge tears. *It's only natural,* he thought. *I know a lot of adults who are too frightened of needles to give blood.*

"OK," the boy said at last. "I'll do it."

Quickly, they prepared the boy for the procedure, which was to take place in the operating room during his sister's surgery. The boy was stoic and grim-faced throughout, bravely accepting every prick and probe he was asked to endure. After the necessary blood had been obtained, the doctors and nurses in the operating room turned their attention to the little girl, whose life hung precariously in the balance just a few feet away from where her older brother lay.

The operation went beautifully, and the surgeons were congratulating each other on their skill and expertise when they were interrupted by a small, weak voice from a table a few feet behind them.

"Hey, Doc," the boy said softly, "is she OK?"

The surgeon who performed the operation beamed. "She's going to be just fine," he said proudly.

"That's great!" The boy was genuinely pleased. Then he grimaced. "So," he said with forced bravado, "when do I croak?"

The doctors looked at each other, puzzled.

"What do you mean?" the head surgeon asked.

"Well, I thought when you took my blood, that meant I was gonna die. So . . . when do I die?"

A respectful silence filled the room as the full significance of the boy's words hit home. He had agreed to give his blood to his little sister with the full expectation that the procedure would result in his own death. Suddenly, the medical feats performed in the operating room seemed less impressive, especially when considered alongside the boy's courage and selfless devotion to something greater than himself—his love for his sister.

It's an inspiring story—but, some may quickly point out, it is just a story. Life isn't really like that, they will say. There's too much selfishness in the world, too much vanity, too much narcissism. It is unrealistic to expect to see such altruism in a world that is dominated by the voices of huge throngs of people shouting "What's in it for me?" —Isn't it?

I don't think so; at least, I choose not to believe that it must be so. Certainly, if we don't at least try to make the world a better place it will never exceed our pessimistic expectations. Discussing the alleged "madness" of his valorous knight Don Quixote, author Don Miguel de Cervantes makes this noteworthy observation: "Maddest of all is he who sees life *as it is* and not *as it should be!*"

Although selfishness, vanity, and narcissism are sad realities of everyday life, they can't dominate us unless we allow them to. If we counter selfishness with selflessness, vanity with compassion, and narcissism with charity for all we can make a difference. Granted, we may only be able to change our own little corner of the world, but it's a start. If more people learn to step through open doors to give of themselves to the world in which they live, we can put enough "little corners" together to form a positive, complete whole.

When we arrive at this point in our journey to authenticity, we discover that some of our priorities have changed. While personal goals and ambitions are important, they often have more to do with helping and serving other people and causes than with achieving for the sake of selfish desires. We are greatly involved with others, just as we were in the Mirrors stage. But now we are influencing others (in positive ways, of course), not being influenced. Rather than being contrasting forces and influences, however, they become a single, unifying force, creating harmony within us as we seek to bring harmony into the world around us through charity.

Some years ago I attended a national conference that attempted to explore how social pressures such as poverty and unemployment have led to a decline of values. During the conference, we spent considerable time in small groups discussing the issues candidly. Throughout those discussions, a recurring theme was sounded:

- "If only I had the money, I would invest in programs to retrain people needing employment."

- "If only I had the authority, I would re-order public policy to give domestic issues a higher priority."

- "If only I had more time and energy, I would personally see to it that nobody in my community went to bed hungry."

One evening as several of my colleagues and I were watching television we noticed a public service announcement asking people to donate $21 per month to provide food and medicine for needy children.

"I could handle $21 per month, or even three times that amount," one of my associates observed. "If only I could be sure that the money would really be used for the children and not for some high-living bureaucrat."

It occurred to me that those two words—"if only"—were being used to justify inaction rather than to explain a choice of action.

Serving others isn't a matter of money, authority, or time; it's a matter of priority. If we care enough and truly value others we will find ways to serve them. We will give what we can give. We will do what we can do. We will find time for that which we value.

A minister I know asked several members of his congregation to help him by making regular, monthly visits to several widows and single mothers that he was concerned about. Most of the visitors did well with the responsibility, but one man almost never made his assigned visits.

"I'm just too busy," he would always say. "I want to help these people, but I just don't have the time. Maybe you should get someone else for the job."

The minister was concerned, and not just for the members of his congregation who weren't being visited. He saw in this man tremendous potential that was going untapped. So one day he called him and invited him to play eighteen holes of golf with him. The man was an avid golfer, and readily agreed to meet the minister at the country club to which he belonged.

They had a wonderful afternoon together, enjoying the sunshine, the game and the fellowship together. After the round, they sat together in the clubhouse sipping soft drinks and mentally replaying the day's most entertaining shots.

"I know how busy you are," the minister said. "I really appreciate your taking an entire afternoon off work just to go golfing with me."

"Oh, I'm happy to do it," the man replied. "You know how much I love to golf. The way I see it, there's always time to golf."

"I guess it's just a matter of priority, isn't it?" the minister asked, a little more thoughtfully.

"Absolutely," the man said. "And golf is the highest priority!"

The man laughed, but the minister didn't. The two men sat for a moment in uncomfortable silence.

"I'm sorry," the man said at last. "I didn't mean to imply that golf is the most important thing in the world to me. It isn't—really. There are lots of things that . . ."

"It's OK," the minister said. "I understand." Again there was heavy silence until the minister put a hand on the other man's arm. "You've got a lot to offer, my friend," he said. "I look forward to the day when people are as important to you as golf is."

The minister was right, and the man knew it. For a few months he made his visits faithfully because he knew that he should, and he was able to provide some meaningful assistance. But it wasn't until he started really loving the people to whom he was assigned—and loving the opportunity to serve them—that he began to reach the potential his minister saw in him.

In the Open Doors stage of living, "if only" is eliminated as an excuse. Instead, we create opportunities to serve by asking ourselves "What if . . . ?" What if we show love to one needy person each day? What if we dedicate a portion of our income, however humble it may be, to help the poor and the hungry? What if we open our homes and hearts to an elderly person who is alone and lonely? The possibilities are endless for anyone who is willing to ignore "if only" and think in terms of "what if?" instead.

When I was an elementary school principal, Timmy was the scourge of the fourth grade. He was out of control most of the time, and none of the teachers wanted him in class. One teacher washed her hands of him after he swallowed all of the guppies in the class aquarium. Another had had enough after he stripped all of the petals from the geranium plants she had brought from home.

"We only have three fourth-grade teachers," I told him as I presented him to his third teacher in less than a month. "Here at our school it's just like in baseball: three strikes and you're out."

It took about two weeks, but finally his teacher brought him back to my office.

"He's yours!" she said. "Don't bring him back into my classroom—ever!"

Timmy and I sat there for a while, just looking at each other. I tried to reach someone at his home, but no one answered the phone. I didn't have anyplace else to take him, and I had work to do.

"You're going to have to sit here with me until I can find someone at home to come and get you," I told him. "You just sit there quietly, and don't disturb me while I work."

For some time he did exactly that. He sat quietly, looking at the floor or out the window. I'm embarrassed to say that I didn't pay much attention to him during that time, so I don't know what else he might have done. I do know that for two hours he didn't say a word. When at last he did speak, it was in a quiet, timid voice.

"Mr. Van Alfen, do you like horses?"

I was a bit surprised at the question. "As a matter of fact, I do," I said. "Why do you ask?"

"I can see a horse book in your bottom drawer," he said. He paused, gathering his courage, then he asked quietly: "Can I look at it?"

I reached for the horse magazine in my drawer. "Do you like horses, too?" I asked as I handed it to him.

"I love horses," he said.

I watched him carefully peruse the magazine. "He isn't such a bad kid," I thought to myself. "Anyone who loves horses can't be all bad. If only he weren't so out of control. If only he could learn to behave. If only his parents would show some interest in his school work."

If only. If only. If only.

"Did you have a horse when you were a little boy?" Timmy asked.

"I grew up on a farm," I told him. "We always had horses. I used to ride my horse all the time."

He looked up from the magazine. "Did you ever ride horses with your Dad?"

"Yes."

"I don't have a Dad," he said, returning his attention to the magazine. "I don't have a horse, either."

As we sat there chatting comfortably about something we both loved, I found the "if only" liabilities turning into "what if" possibilities. What if someone started showing an interest in him? What if he truly believed that someone really cared? What if someone took the time to find out why he was acting the way he was acting and what he needed to turn his life around?

And what if that someone was me?

For the next several days I asked Timmy to come to my office for school. I brought more horse magazines from home, and he enjoyed looking at them. We would talk about horses, which usually led us to talk about my youth, which usually led us to talk about him and his life at home—which, as I suspected, wasn't very pleasant. I began to care a great deal about Timmy, and the more I cared the more I understood. And the more he *knew* that I cared, the more open and responsive he was to my gentle suggestions regarding his behavior.

One day I ran out of horse magazines to bring to Timmy, so I decided it was time to begin moving him back toward the classroom.

"Have you ever read *Black Beauty*?" I asked him.

"No. What's it about?"

"It's a wonderful book about a great horse. I think you'd like it."

"OK," he said. "Bring it to me."

"It's in the library," I said. "I'll take you to it."

"The library?" the boy asked, nervously. "I don't know if I . . ." He hesitated, studying his fingers. At last he told me what I already suspected: "The last time I was in there the librarian told me not to come back."

"Why?"

"I guess I wasn't very good."

"You mean you didn't behave well," I corrected. "Remember what we've talked about, Timmy: you are good; it's just your behavior that is sometimes inappropriate."

"Yeah, that's right."

"Now, do you know how to behave in the library?"

"Yeah," he said. "Be quiet. And don't crawl under the tables."

"You've got it! OK—let's go."

"Right now?" Timmy asked. "But what if the librarian gets mad at me again?"

"She's a nice person, Timmy," I assured him. "As long as you behave yourself I'm sure you'll get along fine."

So we went to the library. Timmy and the librarian kept a suspicious eye on each other while we looked for *Black Beauty*, but they both managed to get through the process without saying anything. When he finished *Black Beauty*, I sent him down to the library by himself to check out *The Black Stallion*. He spent more and more time in the library, reading every book he could find about horses. Eventually he was spending entire days there—without any problems. Soon he was able to return to the classroom.

Timmy helped me see and understand the power of charity by showing me how quickly "if only" can turn into "what if" when mixed with sincere caring and compassion. Like St. Paul says, when it comes to reaching out to others and making a difference in their lives, "charity never faileth."

Some years ago I was working as a counselor in a large, over-crowded metropolitan high school. During this time I became well acquainted with a freshman named David. He had come to us with tremendous potential. He had a good mind and a dynamic personality. His family was prominent and well-off, and his parents made sure that their children had every opportunity and advantage. But halfway through the school year, David was failing every class. He had been absent more times than he had been present. When teachers tried to work with him, he was rude.

I tried everything I could think of to tap this young man's potential. I worked with his parents. I worked with him. We spent hours talking about everything and anything—especially his chrome-covered car, which was the envy of the entire student body. Every effort was met with apathy and indifference.

After several months it became clear that David simply wasn't going to respond. Because he so flagrantly violated school and district attendance policy, I called for a meeting with David and his parents to terminate his association with our school and to refer him to juvenile court. As the group gathered, David took his chair to a corner of my office and sat down in it—facing the corner. I struggled to control the anger and frustration that was building up inside of me. But I couldn't help thinking, "I'm going to be so glad to get rid of this kid. What a waste of time he has been!"

"I can't understand why David has done this to us," David's father blurted out as the meeting began. "We have given him everything he has ever wanted. He has the best car in the city. His closet is full of clothes. We give him $25 a week allowance. Our home has been designed to provide him with a game room and basketball and tennis courts. I don't know what more we could have done for him."

As David's father continued his litany of his son's many advantages and David continued sitting silently in his corner, I found myself thinking that it would be good for David to spend a little time in juvenile hall. Maybe then he would appreciate what he was literally turning his back on.

Suddenly, David stirred from his slumped position. Slowly, he turned to face his father. It wasn't until then that we could see the tears streaming down his cheeks. His shirt was wet with tears, his chest heaving with emotion.

"Sure, I have all that stuff," he said, sobbing. "But when was the last time we went fishing together?"

His father was stunned. "Why, David," he said, "we went fishing last October with Mr. Jackman and his son."

"Yeah, right," he responded with a depth of feeling that was obvious to all. "But you only took me because he wanted to take his son. That was a business deal, Dad, and I was just part of the presentation. You weren't really interested in me."

"But David, what do you want . . ."

"I don't want *anything!* Don't you guys get it? I don't care about all that stuff—the car, the clothes, the house, the money. None of that matters. All I want is for you guys to act like you love me!"

David slumped into his chair in the corner again, still sobbing as if his heart had broken. His father asked me to leave for a few moments to allow the family some time together. When I was finally invited to return, there was a new feeling in the room.

"In the past, we've met with you and asked you to give our son another chance," David's father said. "Now I realize that I need to plead for another chance for David's parents. We love David with all our hearts, but we haven't been acting like it. We've fallen into the trap of equating love with money, and we've tried to prove our love for David by showering him with *things.* But he's smarter than us; he saw what we were doing before we could see it ourselves. He didn't care about our money or any of the things money can provide. All he wants is for us to be what we claim to be, and what we thought we were: a happy, loving, caring family. He says he's willing to give us another chance to actually live our values. Will you give us another chance, too?"

Three and a half years later David graduated from our high school with honors. Today he is a successful family man and is an important part of his father's business.

What made the difference? Was it just the fact that his parents spent more time and energy on their son? Well, that was part of it, to be sure. But the thing that really bothered David was that his parents claimed to love their son and their family, but their actions didn't reflect that charity. Making their actions consistent with their values opened doors of happiness and success for them and for their son.

Chapter Eleven:

The Virtue of Self-Discipline

Hold up your head! You were not made for failure, you were made for victory. Go forward with a joyful confidence in that result sooner or later, and the sooner or later depends mainly on yourself.

—Anne Gilchrist

Self-discipline is the power that we have over ourselves to actually do the things that we value. It is, in essence, the capacity to mold ourselves. And an interesting thing happens in this process: we begin to accept responsibility for our own lives, not as something with which we have been saddled or as a burden forced upon us, but as something we have chosen for ourselves. We are not the result of external forces and influences, but rather, we exist as the result of our chosen reactions to those external influences and decisions we make for ourselves.

Alice had just received a promotion in her chosen career. It was a little surprising, because it was the kind of promotion that usually comes to more mature people in her field. Yet no one doubted that Alice deserved it. She was efficient, effective, and talented, and she was delightful to be around. Rather than being intimidated or jealous, several of her friends and colleagues took her to lunch to celebrate her accomplishment.

"Alice, you're the luckiest person I know!" one of her colleagues teased. "Have you always been so lucky?"

Suddenly, Alice became quite serious. "I don't believe in luck," she said. "In my opinion, the person who gets the opportunity is the person who is prepared when the opportunity comes. I've been preparing myself for this opportunity for a long time."

"But how could you?" another colleague asked sincerely. "You're only twenty-three years old, and you've only been out of college for a couple of years. Other people have been with this company for twenty years and haven't accomplished what you've done. How can you say you've been preparing yourself for this for a long time?"

Alice paused for a moment, carefully choosing her words. "For as long as I can remember," she said, "I've been fascinated by the process of learning. I've read books, I've studied a wide variety of subjects, and I've spent a lot of time thinking about the things that I've learned. And the more I think about things, the more I've learned how to think and how to translate my most creative thoughts into action."

"So that's your secret, huh? Just thinking? What an innovation!"

"Not just thinking," Alice said, chuckling. "It's the entire process of thought. I've discovered that I can create my own joy and happiness—or sadness and misery—through the thoughts I allow myself to think. To a great degree, I can control my life by controlling my thoughts."

"But what do you do when things don't go the way you think they should?" her friend asked.

"Oh, I've been in those situations, just like anyone else," Alice said. "But I've learned that the power of thought can help me work through those situations in a positive way."

"And it's that same power that helped you land that great new promotion?"

"Sort of. Actually, it's the power of thought that has helped me shape who I am and what I do, and that's what got me the promotion—not luck."

"Now, maybe that's more than you wanted to hear," Alice concluded. "But it's what I believe. I control my own destiny through my thoughts. That doesn't mean I can use my thoughts to control the circumstances that surround me. But through my thoughts, I can control how I respond to those circumstances."

As we come to know ourselves and our thoughts better, we better understand the thoughts and actions of others. We develop stronger trust and faith in ourselves and in others. We stop trying to control everything around us and find peace and security in simply controlling ourselves. Such self-control—and such peace—is only possible through the mastery of our thoughts.

Lorenzo is an extraordinarily successful businessman who is widely known to have assisted many people in their time of need. One morning a young mother and her two children came to ask for a little help. Lorenzo's secretary was concerned about his time, and she couldn't help but be troubled by their unkempt appearance. She tried to schedule an appointment for another day.

But it was too late. Lorenzo had heard them. He opened his office door and invited the mother and her children in. They sat and visited for a few minutes. The woman told him that she wasn't there for a handout, but she was hoping there was some work she could do to provide for her children. As she talked, Lorenzo turned to the two children and gestured for them to come to him. They hesitated a moment, then jumped down from their chairs and into his arms. Lorenzo's secretary winced as she thought of those dirty children climbing onto the lap of this elegant, well-dressed man.

Before long, Lorenzo had the woman situated in a new job and the family on their way to a new way of life. After they left, Lorenzo's secretary commented on the family's appearance.

"Wasn't it hard for you to hold those filthy little children on your lap?" she asked.

"Well," he said patiently, "I don't really think of them as filthy little children. I think of them simply as God's children, just like you and me, and I could tell those two children of God needed a hug."

Lorenzo's life was a study in self-discipline, and his actions were dictated by his values. And that's the way it should be for us. If we think of people as being valuable and worthy of our love, then that is how we will treat them. If we look for beauty underneath the accumulated dirt, the matted hair, and the dirty clothes, then we will find it. If we have not learned to think that there is good in all, no matter the color or condition, then we deprive ourselves of some of the greatest opportunities of life. We are what we value, and we value what we think about.

One evening I was relaxing in my study when the telephone rang. The caller said he needed to talk to someone, and my name had been given to him as a person who would listen. We arranged a meeting, during which Bob told me the story of his life. He had been in and out of jail since he was fourteen, a fact that he was quick to blame on abusive parents, unenlightened teachers, incompetent law enforcement officials and an insensitive society. Now, at forty-three, his dreams for the future had been shattered, and he was filled with anger, bitterness, and hopelessness.

"As long as I live," he said, "I will always wonder who I might have been."

Bob is back in prison now—he never learned to accept and respond positively to the consequences of his decisions. But I'll never forget the powerful eloquence of that one simple statement: "I will always wonder who I might have been." Whenever I get the chance I warn people—especially young people—about the potential tragedy of "who I might have been" in each of our lives if we fail to gain self-discipline.

Of course, that's a difficult thing to do if we aren't totally committed to our core values. In this world of quick-fix solutions and instant gratification, self-discipline can be easily rationalized away and commitments can be easily broken. And if you doubt that, consider your most recent set of New Year's resolutions. How many are still in force? How many were still in force by February first? How many were still in force by January second?

See what I mean?

Bob could have led a far different life than he did, but he never developed the self-discipline required to take control of his life. As a result, he looked for people to blame for the state of his life rather than taking personal responsibility for his actions. And so his life is plagued by questions like "I wonder what I might have been," and will continue to be so until he can focus his thoughts on gaining control of his inner consciousness.

Helen, a fifty-year-old business executive, shared with me some of the doubts she was having about herself and her career. Always confident and self-assured, she found that she was focusing more and more attention on relatively insignificant aspects of her life. She noticed, for example, that it required much more time for her to get ready for work in the morning.

"It takes so much more work to get this face looking presentable," she said. "I've thought about plastic surgery—in fact,

I've already had a couple of tucks. But at this point, I'm not sure that there are enough stitches available to repair the damage that the years have done."

Of course, it didn't help that she was surrounded by young, hungry colleagues at work. For the first time in her career, she was beginning to feel threatened by the upwardly mobile junior executives.

"I look at them and I see something very familiar," she said. "I see me—about twenty years ago."

Even the health spa, which had been a sanctuary for her for many years, was becoming a chore. One day while she was working out on the stair-stepper a question occurred to her that she had never asked herself before: "Is this all there is?"

She found herself analyzing a life that had been dedicated to filling her "empty self" with position, beauty, cars, boats, and a beautiful home. Whenever she was unhappy she would buy another car or a bigger boat or take another tuck. But at this point in her life, she was beginning to realize that she had lost control of her life. Outside circumstances completely dominated her behavior rather than her inner virtues. In fact, she wasn't even sure what those virtues were. Because she had never developed the self-discipline needed to take control of the circumstances surrounding her, she was moving into a challenging season of her life as a pawn of external influences and perceptions that now seemed to be turning on her in disconcerting ways.

Self-discipline is about more than just control; to be truly effective, it must come from the heart and soul. Richard Bach's classic, *Jonathan Livingston Seagull* is the story of a seagull who wants to master the art of flying higher, faster, and in greater control. Jonathan would practice flying for hours on end, going ever higher, ever faster, and performing ever more dangerous dives—much to his mother's frustration.

"Why is it so hard for you to be like the rest of the flock, Jon?" she asked. "Why can't you leave low flying to the pelicans, the albatross? Why don't you eat? Son, you're bone and feathers!"

"I don't mind being bone and feathers," Jonathan said. "I just want to know what I can do in the air, and what I can't. That's all. I just want to know."

"If you must study," Jonathan's father said, "then study food and how to get it. This flying business is all very well, but you can't eat a glide, you know. Don't you forget that the reason you fly is to eat."

Jonathan tried to obey his father's counsel for several days, but eventually his need to learn and practice overpowered his attempts to be like all the other seagulls. He returned to his quest and to the exhilaration of doing what he felt he was born to do.

"How much more there is now to living!" Jonathan said after a long, exhausting day of diving. "Instead of our drab slogging back and forth to the fishing boats, there's a reason to life! We can lift ourselves out of ignorance, we can find ourselves as creatures of excellence and intelligence and skill."

Self-discipline, as a virtue in our lives, can do the same for us. It can lift us out of ignorance and help us to become creatures of excellence, intelligence, and skill.

It can also help us become more responsible, as Jonathan found when he was isolated from the flock for non-conformity. "Who is more responsible," he asked, "than a gull who finds and follows a meaning, a higher purpose for life? For a thousand years we have scrabbled after fish heads. But now we have a reason to live—to learn, to discover."

So it is with us. Our self-discipline can take us out of the crowd and set us apart as we follow meaning, gain a higher purpose in life, and find invigorating stimulation to learn and to discover.

Which doesn't necessarily mean life will always be pleasant for us. Because he was so different from other seagulls, Jonathan lived alone. This was frustrating because he was anxious to teach others the things he was learning. For example, he learned that his self-discipline gave him a vision of his creative power. He gained peace and serenity through the strength of inner-control. And he learned the power of being able to control his inner-most thoughts.

Eventually, Jonathan died. But even this was a great adventure for him. At one point in his after-life he looked around and noticed that there weren't many seagulls present.

"Where is everyone?" he asked his companion. "Why aren't there more of us here? Why, where I came from there were . . . thousands of gulls."

"I know," his companion said sadly. "The only answer I can see, Jonathan, is that you are pretty well a one-in-a-million bird. Most of us [came along] forgetting where we had come from, not caring where we were headed, living for the moment."

Self-discipline in our lives may indeed make us one-in-a-million. It will help us learn *who we are*, *where we came from*, and *where we are going*, as Jonathan did. Indeed, we empower ourselves through self-discipline. And as we gain power and control over our lives through self-discipline, we find ourselves yearning to share what we've learned with others. Motivated by kindness and love, we seek out others who are looking for the truths we have already found.

Jonathan certainly felt that way. He wanted to return to the flocks on the seashore, although he wondered if he could handle all of the abuse that would surely be heaped upon him again. The Elder Gull who presided over Jonathan's post-life flock taught him an important principle of self-discipline.

"Don't be harsh on them," the Elder Gull said. "In casting you out, the other gulls have only hurt themselves, and one day they will know this, and one day they will see what you see. Forgive them and help them to understand."

Self-discipline is forgiveness. It is being able to be grateful for personal growth and, through kindness and love, reach out to others who are in need of the information you have to share with them regardless of how they may have treated you.

"The flight of ideas can be as real as the flight of wind and feathers," Jonathan said. "The only difference [between those who have self-discipline and those who don't] is that [those who have it] have begun to understand what they really are and have begun to practice it."

Self-discipline, in the final analysis, is bringing *who we are* and *what we do* into harmony, thus achieving greater authenticity.

Chapter Twelve:

The Virtue of Courage

Freedom is a system based on courage.

—Anonymous

It was a wet, rainy Southern California afternoon. I was working in my office with two assistants. The challenges of the past several months had been overwhelming, and the next few months didn't promise to be any less taxing. Then the telephone rang. The caller introduced herself as a nurse in a hospital emergency room some twenty miles away.

"Your wife has been in a serious car accident," the nurse said. My brain and body went numb. "She's here, and the doctors are working on her. I don't know the full extent of her injuries, but the doctors have asked that you get here as quickly as possible."

My mind raced with a thousand different questions. What happened? Who was to blame? How was she injured? Is she going to be incapacitated? Is she going to live? And, if she doesn't live, what on earth will I do? But, I could only vaguely mumble one of them.

"Is she . . . going to be . . ."

"I can only tell you that she is listed in critical condition at this moment," the nurse said, tersely. "Please hurry."

I left immediately with my assistants, whose deep concern quickly shifted from our work to my wife. Upon our arrival at the hospital, the nurse took me to the examination room where a team of medical professionals was working to save Jeanette's life.

"Her back seems to be pretty badly injured," one of the doctors told me. "Her sternum is crushed, and there are probably other internal injuries that we haven't been able to discover yet. Actually, things could be a lot worse, considering that she was hit head-on by a 65,000-pound tar truck. She was trapped in the car for more than an hour before she could be rescued."

The doctor went back to his work for a moment, leaving me to imagine the horror my wife had experienced. "She's awake," the doctor said. "You can talk to her for a few minutes before we take her into X-ray."

I approached my wife and gently took her hand, now encumbered with needles and tubes. Before I could say anything to her, she spoke.

"I'm so sorry, honey," she said, her voice quiet and choked with emotion. "With all of your other worries, you didn't need this."

Not a word about her pain or her trauma. Nothing about herself at all. Only concern, even under these extraordinary circumstances, for the challenges I was facing.

Challenges, I should add, which suddenly seemed trivial and insignificant.

Before I could help her understand that her well-being was the only thing that mattered to me, the doctors interrupted and wheeled her away to take some X-rays. I waited for what seemed like an eternity, my mind echoing her tender expression of concern for me. As I thought about it, I realized that it shouldn't have surprised me. After all, Jeannette was always caring for others—for me, for our family, for our friends and neighbors. She never really worried much about herself. And now, at a time when she could justifiably feel sorry for her condition and seek sympathy for her tragedy, she was only concerned for the added burden her accident would place upon me.

Thankfully, she recovered beautifully from her injuries. But I've never forgotten the powerful lesson she taught me in that California hospital.

The true essence of who we really are comes forward in times of trial. When push comes to shove, we can't hide behind pretense or superficial reflections of reality. We can only open up ourselves and let the truth come through. It is in that truth that we find the internal power and strength we seek, especially if we have reached the Open Doors stage of our journey to authenticity. For if *who we are* and *what we do* are harmonious in our lives, they combine to focus our collective energy on our trials in much the same way that a magnifying glass gathers and focuses the burning rays of the sun. Without the disruptions and distractions of insecurity, we can gather strength and confidence from the clear vision provided by our thoughts, virtues, and beliefs.

In a very real way, life is like a ship's voyage. It begins in the Mirrors stage, where we can, by coming to see ourselves reflected from a variety of perspectives, build a seaworthy craft. In the Windows stage, we can obtain a rudder of vision, hope, and dreams that can provide guidance, direction, and purpose. But a fine ship and a well-designed rudder are pretty useless without some form of energy to drive the boat. That is what we obtain through courage: internal power, focused on the energizing vision of core values and beliefs. It is only with that kind of highly developed power, carefully honed by our thoughts and actions, that we can hope to sail headlong into the waves of adversity and not be swamped.

In fact, adversity brings out the true internal self. During times of crisis, we tend to see our actual goals more clearly, and contradictory and inessential choices become less intrusive. At such times, it almost seems to be easier to master the challenges of circumstance and develop a clarity of purpose we may have lacked before.

According to behavioral scientists, courage is one of the most admired characteristics people look for in others. If you ask me, that's just as it should be. Of all the virtues we can learn, no trait is more useful and more likely to improve the quality of our lives than the ability to transform adversity into a stimulating challenge. To admire this quality means we pay attention to those who embody it, and are therefore likely to attempt to emulate them as the need arises. For this reason, admiring courage is in itself a positive adaptive trait.

Courage is best learned through filling the "empty self" with deeply held virtues that can be called upon when needed. Modeling is one of the most effective ways to teach or learn this virtue. Mental models obtained through associating with or learning about people who have this inner strength is a valuable way to develop courage. For example, I have learned much from the following story, told to me by an aging war veteran who witnessed the event. He handed out a written treatment as follows:

> If you should happen to find yourself in self-pity, you might consider the life of Michael J. Dowling.

When but a young man of fourteen, Michael was overcome by a blizzard in Michigan. Before his parents discovered him, he was frostbitten so badly that he had to undergo amputation of his limbs. His right leg was amputated almost to the hip; his left leg above the knee; his right arm was amputated as well as his left hand.

Can you guess the consequences? He went to the board of County Commissioners and asked for a loan to educate himself, with the promise that he would pay back every cent he borrowed.

During World War I, Michael Dowling became president of one of the largest banks in St. Paul, Minnesota, but he left his position and went to Europe to help build soldiers' morale.

On one occasion in London he lectured a group of wounded, discouraged soldiers. During his speech he minimized their wounded condition. He refused to sympathize with them, and the wounded men eventually began to jeer him.

Then Michael Dowling began walking toward the steps, still reminding the wounded soldiers how fortunate they were. As the soldiers vented their anger toward him, he sat down and removed his right leg. The soldiers quieted somewhat. When he took off his left leg there was sudden and complete silence. Then he removed his right arm and his left hand. He sat there on the stage, just a stump of a body—and a bank president and the father of five.

Michael Dowling proved something to everyone with a handicap: it's not the handicap that causes failure, but the lack of courage to overcome the handicap.

One of the hallmarks of the Open Door person is that they have come to understand themselves and their relationships with others, and they have developed their faith sufficiently to be able to cope with adversity in a serene, confident way. People in the Open Doors stage have the advantage of being able to deal with adversity from a position of power because they know and understand that even though they can't always choose the challenges that will come into their lives, they can choose how they will react to those challenges. And thus they maintain a sense of control and order, even under the most uncontrolled and disorganized circumstances.

When we look at life as a creative opportunity, we see even in adversity possibilities for growth. When we learn to find the serenity and joy possible in the experiences of each moment without spending all of our time trying to label those experiences as "good" or "bad," we will have greater inner-strength to face the kinds of adversity we will all deal with at one time or another. Because we understand that all experiences can, if managed properly, eventually work to our advantage, we can accept life on its own terms and focus our time and attention on moving forward—courageously.

Great power is manifest in people's lives when they begin to realize that they are not under the control of outside circumstances, but are truly the creators of their own respective destinies. Such power only comes, however, as a basic core of virtues fills the "empty self" and life is motivated by intrinsic forces, as opposed to extrinsic forces.

While trying to teach this important principle to a therapy group comprised of young men and women, the therapist told a story written by Margaret White Eggleston about an ancient Spaniard who became very angry with a Moor over the subject of religion.

"My God would not have one such as you live," the Spaniard cried as he drew his sword. "Die, you coward!"

The Spaniard thrust his blade into the startled Moor, killing him instantly. As the Moor's body crumpled to the roadside, the Spaniard saw a group of people coming down the road. The people could see what was happening, and they began to run toward the Spaniard. Frightened, he hurried down the road ahead of the angry mob. Because he knew the countryside better than they, he was able to elude them. He dropped over a wall into the garden of a wealthy Moor. Seeing the old man working among his beautiful flowers, he ran to him and fell on his knees.

"In my haste I have killed a man who loved not God," he said. "Please save me from the mob at the gates. I have done only what seemed right. Save me, I beg of you."

"If thou has done wrong, thou should surely be punished," said the old man. "But it is not for me or for a mob to judge and punish thee. I will share with thee this peach which I have picked from the tree. When we have eaten together, thou canst be assured of my protection. When night cometh, I will come unto thee."

He locked the Spaniard in his garden house and went to sit on his porch. He had hardly seated himself when he heard the sound of many people outside his home. They knocked at his gate and his servant admitted them.

"What hast thou here?" he asked as they entered his garden.

"We have the body of thy son, thine only son," said a member of the mob. "He hath been killed by a Spaniard not far from thine own door. Let us leave him here and go quickly, that we may join in the search for the man who wronged thee."

Without a word he let them depart; then he shut himself in his room and fell to the ground, sobbing. His son was the one great joy of his life. He was beloved by all who knew him. But now he was dead, and in his garden house sat the very man who, by his own admission, had killed him. He had only to say the word, and the mob would take the murderer away and avenge his son's death—harshly. But he had promised protection to the man. They had eaten together. To seek vengeance upon him was unthinkable, for he was a Moor.

All day he paced back and forth in the room overlooking the sea, now black with wind and rain. In his soul was a great storm. As mourners gathered to offer comfort, they watched the old man in anguish. "Behold, how he loved him!" they said softly to each other.

When at last the night fell, he asked his servants to return to their own homes, as he wished to be left alone in his grief. When the last had gone, he went to the garden house and slowly unlocked the door. As the grateful Spaniard emerged and began to express his thanks, the Moor silenced him with an enraged look that made the younger man tremble.

"Thou art a Christian, yet thou hast killed my only son in thine anger," the old man bellowed. "His body lieth in my house. Thou shouldst be severely punished. But I have eaten with thee. I gave thee my word, and my word shall not be broken. I leave thee to thine own God, believing that thou must answer to him for the breaking of his own law. Come!"

With trembling footsteps the old man led the Spaniard to the street where one of his fastest horses was ready for him to mount.

"Go!" said the father. "Go far while the night may be a help unto thee. God is just and God is good. I thank him that I have no load such as thine to carry. 'Tis easier to carry sorrow than shame. My son's memory shall be to me as the sunlight and the moonlight, as the fragrance of the violet and the beauty of the rose, as the cooling breeze on a weary day. Thou hast taken his life, but couldst not take away what he has been to his father. That is mine. Go, and may thine anger never again cause thee to break the law of thy God. Go!"

As the sound of the swiftly moving horse's hooves died away, the old man went again to stand by the bier of his son—his only son.

"Better thou art here than there, my son," he said. "And thy father hath still kept the faith that he taught unto thee."

After the therapist told the story, the reactions from the members of her group ran the gamut from tears of sorrow to anger and the recommendation to "kill him." During the course of the lively discussion that followed, the young people wrestled with significant questions: what kind of inner-strength would it take to make the decision the old man made? What kind of insights into life and relationships did the old man have to create the courage, under these extreme conditions, to stay true to his convictions? And what must we do to become the kind of people who could say, "Better thou art here than there, my son" and "Thy father hath still kept the faith that he taught unto thee."

What a powerful model through story to teach the virtue of courage!

Courage is characterized by creativity, optimism, and wholeness. It requires courage to be a creative force. In *Leadership and the New Science*, Margaret J. Wheatley introduces her "field theory," in which one envisions an imaginary field or space around each individual or organization. "I can imagine an invisible customer service field filling the spaces of those stores we visited," Wheatley writes. "The field didn't just drift into the store. In each of those stores there was a manager who, together with employees, took time to fill the store space with clear messages about how he or she wanted customers to be served."

Applying this principle to our lives, let's assume that each of us has a space or field of influence. We can either fill that field with meaningful behaviors and messages, or the natural flow of society will fill it with the "other-directed empty self" influence. It takes courage to step into that space and boldly create a vision of hope and dream. It takes courage to be a model of virtue, and to fill the field around you with a vision of goodness and hope, especially when the forces pushing back into that field are extrinsic factors of physical appetite, power and worldly possessions. It takes courage to permeate your "space" with your central core of virtues.

But the fact is, that space must be filled with something. How much better for us and for those around us if it is filled with *authentic*, whole-sighted perspectives of our virtues and values. Since we are going to be modeling messages one way or another, I would rather model the virtues by which I choose to live. After we achieve serenity through control of our consciousness, our quest becomes one of filling the field around us with this serenity. This takes courage.

Becoming a creative influence carries with it the responsibility of continuous growth and the striving to continuously learn. Courage is the basic virtue for all of us as we continue to grow and to move ahead. It is, as author Ellen Glasgow, wrote, "the only lasting virtue." Courage is an inward quality, a way of relating to one's self and one's possibilities. As we develop the courage to deal with ourselves, we can with much greater equanimity meet the threats of the external situations that confront us. As a result, courage is the basis of any creative relationship.

Courage and creativity are inseparably connected. Every act of genuine creativity requires a higher level of self-awareness and control over inner-consciousness. It takes greater courage to preserve inner freedom than to stand defiantly for outer freedom. The hallmark of courage in our age of conformity is the capacity to stand alone on one's own convictions.

A few years ago you could see the slogan, "Just Say No," on bumper stickers, windows and posters just about everywhere you looked. Everyone was talking about teaching our young people to "just say no" to drug abuse and other negative behaviors. I once attended a school symposium on substance abuse and heard a teenager named Alice take issue with the concept.

"That's a great slogan," she said. "It sounds so easy. But when you're out there, it's a whole different thing.

"Do you know what it's like to be ostracized because you're the 'goodie-goodie?'" Alice continued. "I tried it. Do you know what it's like to be alone in high school, with no friends, not even the kids who don't do drugs? Do you know how it feels to have nobody trust you? Do you know what you're asking us to do when you ask us to 'just say no'?"

She looked around the room at the adults. "You make it sound so easy," she said. "Well, it isn't. I can stay away from drugs and stuff, which is what I know I should do, or I can have friends. Those are my choices: I can mess around a little, or I can be isolated. And what I want to know is, why should I, when even my parents don't 'say no'?"

Those are tough questions—for Alice and for the rest of us. It isn't easy to take a stand based on our virtues, especially when such a stand places us squarely in the minority—or even all alone. Where does the courage come from to stand alone? What would you say to Alice?

Rudyard Kipling wrote of this kind of courage in his classic poem, "If":

If you can keep your head when all about you
Are losing theirs and blaming it on you;
If you can trust yourself when all men doubt you,
But make allowance for their doubting, too;
If you can wait and not be tired by waiting,
Or, being lied about, don't deal in lies,
Or, being hated, don't give way to hating,
And yet don't look too good, nor talk too wise;

If you can dream—and not make dreams your master;
If you can think—and not make thoughts your aim;
If you can meet with triumph and disaster
And treat those two impostors just the same;
If you can bear to hear the truth you've spoken
Twisted by knaves to make a trap for fools,
Or watch the things you gave your life to broken,
And stoop to build 'em up with worn-out tools;

If you can make one heap of all your winnings
And risk it on one turn of pitch-and-toss,
And lose, and start again at your beginnings
And never breathe a word about your loss;
If you can force your heart and nerve and sinew
To serve your turn long after they are gone,
And so hold on when there is nothing in you
Except the Will which says to them: "Hold on!"

If you can talk with crowds and keep your virtue,
Or walk with kings—not lose the common touch;
If neither foes nor loving friends can hurt you;
If all men count with you, but none too much;
If you can fill the unforgiving minute
With sixty seconds worth of distance run —
Yours is the Earth and everything that's in it,
And—which is more—you'll be a Man, my son!

There are powerful examples of virtue-driven courage in history for Alice to study and be guided by: Rosa Parks on that evening in December, 1955, when she refused to move to the back of the bus; Pierre and Marie Curie, the French chemists and physicists who were willing to risk deathly illness in order to find life-saving cures for disease; and Susan B. Anthony, who endured incredible persecution and hardship to lead the ultimately victorious fight for women's suffrage.

If I could speak to Alice today, I would tell her that even though her situation is challenging, it is far from hopeless. You have a choice, Alice! The models of courage are there for you! Said Eleanor Roosevelt, a pretty good example of courage herself: "You gain strength, courage, and confidence by every experience in which you really stop to look fear in the face. You are able to say to yourself, 'I lived through this horror. I can take the next thing that comes along.' You must do the thing you think you cannot do."

What a virtue—the virtue of courage!

Part Four

Serendipity

Synergism

and

Symbiosis

Chapter Thirteen:

Serendipity

Do the thing—and you shall have the power, but they who do not the thing have not the power.

—Ralph Waldo Emerson

So there you have it: my concept of attaining authenticity. Your challenge is to consider these ideas, sift through them carefully, and if you find they have merit, give them a try. Of course, we often face that challenge, don't we. We read a thoughtful book, we hear an inspiring sermon and we begin thinking many hopeful thoughts. The problem we encounter is putting those hopeful thoughts into action.

Like they say in the athletic shoe advertisements: "Just do it!"

Disraeli taught that "genius is the power to make continuous effort." One of the most exciting ideas to grow out of our continuous effort is the principle of serendipity. One day as I sat in the waiting room at a local heating fuel company, I read a little document about the word "serendipity." The document did not have a reference to a source, but the thought was exciting. It went something like this:

The word comes to us from Horace Walpole, Earl of Oxford and a member of Parliament. On a cold and foggy winter's day, January 28, 1754, he wrote a letter to Sir Horace Mann to the effect that an old Persian fairy tale had made a profound impression on his life.

The tale was about the Three Princes of Serendip (Serendip was an ancient name for Ceylon). These three young noblemen, while traveling through the world, rarely found the treasures they were looking for, but continually ran into other treasures equally great or even greater, which they were not seeking. In looking for one thing they found something else. And it dawned on them that this was one of life's wonderful tricks. When they realized this, they got an entirely new slant on life; that every day resulted in some new and thrilling experience.

Even though their conscious goals eluded them, they were more than rewarded with their wayside discoveries, and soon it was as if an unseen power and guidance seemed to know, better than they knew, what was best for them in the long run of search and discovery.

And Walpole went on to write that this was what often happened to him. He said, "It is as if I had a talisman that comes to my aid in the nick of time."

But there's a trick to this business of having happy and serendipitous things happen to you: you must be on a quest of some kind. You must be active and in the swim of things . . . you need to be searching, or studying, or working toward a goal of some kind.

Serendipitous things happen to people who expect more good than bad in life and who stick with what they're doing when the going gets rough. In fact, it's just at that particular time that serendipity most often steps into the picture. The scientist, who has for years been working for one thing, suddenly discovers something completely different, but even more wonderful. Penicillin was discovered in this way . . . as were thousands of other things. The Americas were discovered while looking for a new route to India. That's serendipity. But it only happens to those who are out looking for something, who are on a quest of some kind, in some field.

Each of us must have a quest. We must have a vision, or a mental model, of what it is that we are seeking. And then we must "do it"— work. And then keep right on working. The outcome may not be exactly what we set out to achieve, but, as Nightingale described, we will often discover something even better along the way.

A friend of mine, Jake, was known throughout the county as an outstanding farmer. One year at the state fair he received the Farmer of the Year award from the state Farm Bureau. As the award was presented, the public official who was making the presentation asked Jake to share with the group the secret of his success. Jake, a man of few words, paused for a moment. Then he said something simple and profound.

"All I can tell you to do," he said, "is just keep hoein'."

The same principle applies to our efforts to bring *who we are* and *what we do* into greater harmony. We just need to keep on hoein'.

Sterling W. Sil, one of the nation's leading insurance executives and a prominent religious leader, wrote a book called *How to Personally Profit from the Laws of Success.* In it he shared a story about a man who was being interviewed about his success in business.

"How did you come to be so successful?" the interviewer asked.

"I've always been very successful—even as a boy," the businessman replied. "I remember how my friends and I used to go out hunting for bird eggs. I could always find more eggs than any of the other boys."

"Did you know a secret that the other boys didn't know?"

"No," the businessman said. "I just looked under more bushes than anyone else."

Far too many of us give up too early on our quests. We must learn to "keep hoein'." "Do it!" should be our motto in every pursuit, but especially this one. Continual effort toward the realization of our dreams and goals is the key to success for all people everywhere.

But it really does require effort. Sometimes difficulties come along that make discontinuing our quest seem not only desirable, but necessary. As Samuel Johnson said, "Adversity has ever been considered the state in which a man most easily becomes acquainted with himself." Those who are able to work their way through adversity are the only ones who are able to reach the ultimate, desired goal.

Writing this book has reinforced that concept for me. To tell you the truth, I've wanted to quit several times during the process of putting all of this material together. Each time I hit a dead end I seriously considered throwing in the towel. But, I learned that if I could just force myself to sit down in front of my word processor, eventually a thought would come to mind. One bit of reading would lead inevitably to another. As I worked out the thought, it eventually became an idea that I could write down with the hope of benefiting others. The best way to accomplish nothing on this book was to do nothing. When I tried to actually do something toward completing this project, inevitably something good happened—even if it wasn't exactly what I had planned or anticipated—that's serendipity.

When Clarice arrived at the university to begin her Ph.D. fellowship, she was excited about the opportunity that lay before her. The fellowship was fully funded, and she was to complete it while working with one of the nation's leading experts in the field of organizational behavior. Her vision was that this experience would serve as a starting point for a career that would have her working with a variety of organizations, helping them work more effectively with the individuals within the organization.

When she reported to the professor on the first day of class, she was taken to a large quonset hut, where she met the crew of a new military aircraft that was under development. Next she was shown the large, complex instrument panel that controlled the plane. The professor then described her assignment: for the next two years she would spend her days trying to find the most effective placement for each of the dials on the instrument panel based on hundreds of simulated action conditions. It was a psycho-motor study, with much at stake in terms of lives and machinery.

Clarice was both surprised and disappointed. She wanted to work with people and the processes of human growth and development. She had no interest in instruments or bombers or even bomber crews. She asked the professor if she had any options.

"Yes, you have two," the professor said. "Take it or leave it. This fellowship is being provided to do this work. If you can't do the work, then someone else will have the fellowship."

Clarice just couldn't see herself studying that panel all day every day for two years, so she turned it down. She walked away from the quonset hut with no fellowship and severely damaged relations with the professor who held the key to her future.

For hours Clarice roamed the campus, trying to decide what to do. She walked through building after building, paying little attention to the various disciplines housed within each. Finally, a distinguished looking gentleman stopped her.

"You look like you need to talk to someone," the gentleman said.

"Does it show that much?" Clarice asked.

"Yes, it does. Now tell me—how can I be of help?"

Clarice spilled out her frustrations. They talked about her dilemma, and explored some possible alternatives. The man even asked for a reference to one of Clarice's previous teachers, who was immediately called for insight and information. Finally the man introduced himself to Clarice. He was Dr. Malous, the chairman of the university's Educational Psychology Department.

"It just so happens that we have an available fellowship, comparable to the one you just left behind," Dr. Malous said. "I think this work will be more to your liking, and it's yours if you want it."

Clarice gratefully accepted—and changed the course of her life.

Was it luck? Chance? No! The principle of serendipity was at work in Clarice's life. She was prepared, she had worked hard in her studies, and she was ready to step through whichever doors opened in her behalf.

The same applies for us. We all just need to keep doing our best, and to follow the advice our mothers gave us: "Do your best, be good, and work hard."

Not necessarily in that order.

Still, it's important to understand what we have to do to allow serendipity to have an influence on our lives. First, we must overcome the controlling influence of *who others think we are* and develop a healthy vision of *who we think we can become.*

We must also have a mental model of what we want to have happen in our lives, which means we must at least be in the Windows stage of living. We must be learning and valuing, with both eyes focused on the big picture while we try to put the pieces of the puzzle together.

The key, however, is that we keep on working as we keep our vision in mind. As our quest continues, events and people will alter our mental models and shift the focus of our direction. Sometimes we will have to deal with discouragement, frustration, anxiety, stress, and depression. All of these obstacles can be overcome, as long as we keep remembering that we are the creators of our own destiny.

As long as we keep working. Or hoeing, as the case may be.

In *Leadership and the New Science,* Dr. Margaret Wheatley teaches academic principles that support the real-life insight of my farmer friend Jake. According to Dr. Wheatley, it is important that we learn to live with chaos, for it is out of understanding fluctuations, disorder and change that we begin to get a glimpse of a new way in our quest. We learn the elements of how to create within a universe that is in a constant state of movement. This movement is always toward holism, toward understanding and giving primary value to relationships that exist among seemingly disparate parts.

The basic point for us is that a living system is constantly changing. It is a never-resting process that constantly seeks its own self-renewal. If we are to enter into the creative role that the Open Doors stage provides for us—and that Dr. Wheatley's chaos theory suggests—something needs to happen to each of us individually that allows us to accept and prosper in a state of flux.

And that isn't easy for most of us. Indeed, it is impossible to deal with the uncertainty of creating within an unstructured environment if we haven't first dealt with our inner self. People in the Mirrors stage cannot deal with the ambiguities presented by chaos. Only when we have established a basic core of inner virtues that give us control of our consciousness can we deal with the uncertainties of our lives, and it is only at this point that we can begin to take advantage of serendipitous opportunities as they present themselves.

Consider the following hypothetical situation: A family consisting of father, mother and two children are living together in a home that is increasingly filled with contention. Disputes over family governance are frequent. Grades in school are going down. Productivity in all aspects of life are affected by the physical and emotional chaos that is going on in the home.

What are we going to do?

The typical approach is for the parents to tighten control of the children's lives. No play until homework is checked, earlier bed times, punishments for arguing and other contentious activities. Such controls are common responses to family chaos. As parents, we attempt to order the external circumstances as a way of controlling external influences and attitudes and solving problems.

But what if our hypothetical family takes another approach? What if the parents enter into a conversation with their children and propose that the family unite to take on a quest.

"A quest?" the children respond.

"That's right—a quest," the father says. "We're going to go in search of more trust, more gratitude, more charity, more self-discipline, and more courage."

"Oh, brother," the children say, rolling their eyes and folding their arms.

"What's the matter?" the mother asks. "Don't you want us to trust you?"

"Well, yes," says one child. "But I don't think . . ."

"And don't you want us to be grateful for your contributions around here?" the father asks.

"Sure," the other child says. "It just sounds . . ."

"And don't you want us all to love each other, and to have self-discipline and courage?" the mother asks.

"Of course," the first child says. "But a quest? Give me a break."

"I think it sounds fun!" the father says.

"I think it sounds dorky!" the second child says.

OK—so maybe such a conversation won't be easy at first. We're talking about significant changes in family dynamics. It will require time and considerable patience to get everyone enthused about undertaking the quest. But if our hypothetical parents are open, honest, and persistent, and are willing to share feelings, stories, and experiences and model related behaviors, I believe it can happen.

Of course, we're not really talking about just one conversation, are we? We're talking about life-long changes that will require our time and attention for the rest of our lives. Our quest would not be built on isolated events, but on meanings. *who we are* and *what we do* would be central to this quest. Events would be discussed and shared, but they would not be seen as the end result of our efforts. Since the real goal of the quest will be to build long-term inner-strength in each group member, individual short-term events—both bad and good—would be considered part of the process, not an end in itself.

So when a child comes home with a bad grade report, it is viewed as a step in the journey—not the end of the world. Instead of lecturing and punishing, the conversation focuses on educational goals and the kind of learner we want someday to become. And the result of the conversation, hopefully, is increased understanding, awareness, and self-esteem, as opposed to the heightened conflict and pain that always seems to accompany the dictatorial approach.

An interesting thing begins to happen as a result of such conversations. Greater trust develops through truthful sharing, and gratitude for what we have dominates the feeling in the house. Love begins to prevail in the home. Self-control permeates behavior and the courage to face the adversity and chaos of every day living gains strength.

This doesn't happen through carefully planned and structured events. It happens over time, on a journey with a quest, during the course of which serendipitous events and opportunities have a pronounced influence upon the process of growth. While there will be bumps along the way in the form of complications and concerns, as we gain greater meaning within each individual and collective strength in family relationships we will be able to absorb the bumps and continue our journey safely—together.

The same concept also applies to relationships in the work place, the neighborhood, the community, and the church with serendipitous potential existing in every direction. In his fun and insightful song "Dig Another Well," Paul Overstreet teaches this valuable lesson:

Well, Ike had a blessing from the Lord up above.
Gave him a beautiful woman to love,
A place to live, a nice little farm,
Two good legs and two good arms.

Well, the devil came sneaking around one night
And decided he would do a little evil to Ike.
Figured he would hit old Ike where it hurts,
So he filled up all of Ike's wells with dirt.

When Ike went out for his morning drink
He got a dipper full of dirt and his heart did sink.
But he knew it was the devil so he said with a grin,
"God blessed me once, he can do it again."

So when the rains don't fall and the crops all fail,
And the cows ain't putting any milk in the pail,
Don't sit around waitin' for a check in the mail,
Just pick up the shovel and dig another well.

Now, me and old Ike got a lot in common:
The Lord blessed me with a beautiful woman,
He gave me a job and he gave me a home,
And he gave me a well to call my own.

When I go out for my morning drink
And get a dipper full of dirt, my heart does sink.
But I think of old Ike and I have to grin,
"God blessed me once, and he can do it again.

Well, the Good Book say Ike finally won.
The devil got tired and he left him alone.
Because the Good Book tells me what to do.
Pick up the shovel and dig another well.

In some respects our ancestors seemed to innately understand this concept better than we do. While reading some pioneer history recently I came upon the story of an insightful man named Jacob, who was nearly overcome with grief when his young wife died on their journey to the American West. As he gently placed the last stone on the shallow grave he had dug for his beloved wife, Elizabeth, he wanted to lie down beside her and sleep.

"Papa?"

The voice of his eight-year-old son, Benjamin, brought him back to the hard realities of life on the trail with a pioneer wagon train.

"Yes, Ben?"

"I made this." The boy handed his father a flat piece of wood, upon which he had written a single word— "Mama"— with a blackened stick from the camp fire. A wave of emotion swept over Jacob as he remembered how hard Elizabeth had worked to teach Ben to read and write.

"That's a fine marker, Son," Jacob said at last. "Your Mama'd be proud to have it."

The boy smiled bravely through moist, reddened eyes, and together father and son attached the marker to the grave as a final tribute to the woman they both loved.

"Excuse me, Jacob."

Both Jacob and Benjamin turned to see the wagon master, his hat in his hand. For the first time Jacob was aware of the activity behind him, as settlers were finishing breakfast and packing their covered wagons in preparation for another day on their journey.

"I know this is a hard time," the wagon master said softly. "But we need to be goin'."

"We can't go!" Benjamin shouted. "Tell 'im, Papa! We can't just go and leave Mama here!"

The wagon master looked at the boy, then at Jacob, who slowly knelt to speak to his son.

"Ben," he said. "We've got to move on."

"But, Papa, Mama . . ."

"Nobody loved your Mama more than me," Jacob said. "But she wanted us to make a good life for ourselves. We can't do that here. We've got to move on."

The boy stared at his mother's grave. Somehow, deep down inside, he knew his father was right. They would have to move on. But not today. "Can't we wait a few days?" he asked. "We can catch up to the others later."

Jacob shook his head slowly. "I'm sorry, Son," he said, "but in a few days the rest of the company will be so far ahead we'll never catch up. And without them we can't survive."

The boy's chin quivered slightly. He looked at his father and then at the wagon master, who squatted so he could face him eye-to-eye.

"Ben," he asked, "you remember a few days back when we were goin' through that rough stretch on the trail?"

The boy nodded.

"Some said we should turn back," the older man said. "Others said we should stop a while, like maybe the trail would change in a day or two. But do you remember what we did?"

"We just . . . kept a-goin'."

"That's right. And we made it, didn't we? It was a tough pull, but we just kept pluggin' along and we got through it." He paused, then he added: "Just like I figure you and your Pa'll make it through this rough stretch of road you're on—if you just keep a-goin'."

And that's what they did: they kept a-goin'. They moved on; and they survived.

The same is true for us today when we encounter rough stretches along the road of life. No matter how much we may want to quit or turn back or give in to the pressures, most of the time the best thing we can do is just keep a-goin'. We may have to slow our pace from time to time, and occasionally we may even have to change directions. But as long as we just keep pluggin' along, eventually we'll get through it. And we'll survive—authentically.

The serendipitous journey in its most basic form is a conversation. And not just any conversation. Recently my wife said to me, "Curtis, when are we going to sit down and talk?"

The question caught me a little off-guard. "Well," I said, "we talk all the time."

"I know—we talk," she said. "We talk about this event and that situation. But that isn't what I'm asking. When are we going to sit down and have a real conversation about what is happening in our lives?"

"What do you mean?" I asked, concerned. "What's happening?"

"I don't know," she said. "That's the point. Where are we going? What are we doing? And when are we going to do the things that you teach and write about?"

"We do it all the time," I said. "Don't we?"

"We used to," she said. "But lately it seems that our conversations are just correlation meetings, where we coordinate our schedules and activities and catch up on the latest bits of news and information. We're not really examining our lives. We're not really moving in a specific direction. We're just . . . existing. I want to know: is this all there is?"

It seems as if I've heard that question posed before. But it had been a long time since I'd considered it with regards to my own life and most valued relationships. My wife had sounded an important wake-up call—for me and for us.

Studies show that the typical father has about two minutes of conversation with his children each day. Is it any wonder that these children seek meaning and validation elsewhere? In a society that is dominated by "other-directed empty self" living, they find their virtues in the external gratification that is glamorized for them in the media and in the Mirrors-oriented models they see all around them. That's why the question, "When are we going to sit down and talk?" is such a powerful question.

Conversation can be a serendipitous journey for most of us. Recently I asked a friend of mine about his neighbors.

"You know," he said, "I don't know much about them."

"Oh," I said. "Did they just move in?"

"Yeah," he said. "Well . . . about eight years ago."

Eight years without meaningful communication. Can there be any sense of community without conversation?

During the past ten years I have conducted research into the kinds of things we talk about in our organizations. I have examined meeting transcripts, notes, and minutes to determine how much time is spent on institutional discussion (rules, regulations, and structured events) as compared to individual matters (the needs wants and feelings of people within the organizational setting). My findings have been quite stunning. More than ninety-eight percent of the time in these meetings is spent on the institutional matters, while only two percent of the discussion focuses on the heart of the institution's future—its people.

Nor is this simply a business phenomenon. One of the activities I require of my college students is journal-keeping. Throughout a limited period of time, I ask them to record their thoughts and feelings every half hour. Then at the end of the day, I ask them to write a one paragraph summary of their thoughts of the day, focusing on the mix of institutional-type thoughts and thoughts that center on feeling, valuing, and spending time on the individual. I guess the assignment stems from my father's thought: "Tell me what you think about when you don't have to think, and I'll tell you what you are."

Not too long ago a forty-five-year-old doctoral candidate came into my office, threw his journal on my desk and proclaimed: "You can flunk me if you must, but I'm not keeping this journal any longer!"

"Well, your grade isn't dependent upon the journal, so you can quit writing in it if you wish," I said. "But I would like to talk to you about it."

"No!" he said vehemently. "I don't even want to think about this ridiculous activity any more, much less talk about it." Then he stormed out of my office.

During the next few weeks he was noticeably subdued in class as we discussed the role of thoughts, conversation, and our process of gaining control over our inner-consciousness while becoming *authentic* people. Then one day, about three weeks after he left his journal on my desk, he dropped by my office again. This time he wanted to talk.

"The two weeks I kept the journal were very disturbing to me," he confided. "I've always thought of myself as a 'people person' who valued people over institutional demands. And I always considered my thoughts to be wholesome, positive, and constructive. But as I recorded my thoughts I discovered that there is a considerable distance between *who I thought I was* and *what I actually do*. I'm a hypocrite. I'm distressed at what I think about when I don't have to think. I'm controlled by events, and I control others with events. I seldom enter into real conversation with people, especially those I love most. I talk to people, but I don't really converse."

He glanced at his journal, which had been occupying a corner of my desk ever since he tossed it there three weeks earlier. "Can I have my journal back?" he asked, a little sheepishly. "I need to continue on this journey."

This student's experience is not uncommon. As we begin to look at *who we are*, we quickly see opportunities for growth. As we gain control over our inner-consciousness, the process of developing virtues open new horizons of learning. And as this learning dynamic takes place in our lives, we become more capable of dealing with the unknown chaos of the processes of life and become creators of our own destiny.

As Dr. Wheatley says, "homeostasis, balance, and equilibrium—these are temporary states. What endures is process—dynamic, adaptive, creative."

This process is serendipity. It isn't enough just to be on the quest; you've got to be ready to deal with changes, adjustments, and uncertainty. With a base of virtues and the attitudes of optimism, faith, hope, and charity we can proceed on our serendipitous journey by entering into conversations that will allow us to develop relationships of truth through truth, gratitude, charity, self-discipline, and courage.

In the final analysis, our quest is a search for meaning and value. For example, imagine a row of chairs in front of you filled with disadvantaged people. The first chair is occupied by a man who was tongue-tied at birth, the second person is blind, the third is deaf and the fourth stammers when he tries to speak.

It would be easy to look at that group and think, "Boy, am I glad I don't teach Special Ed." But if you probe a little bit—have a conversation and open yourself to these people—you'll discover that the one who was tongue-tied at birth was Demosthenes, who became the greatest orator in Greece. The blind man is Milton, who wrote "Paradise Lost." Next to him is Beethoven, who wrote some of his best music after he lost his hearing. And the fourth member of the group is Samuel Clemens, also known as Mark Twain, who became famous when he relied on his writing instead of his stammering tongue for communication.

The thing that helped these disadvantaged people to become remarkably successful is they played to their strengths and refused to be limited by the challenges life tossed their way. They kept hoein'. They kept a-goin'. They picked up a shovel and dug another well.

And the rest, as they say, is serendipity.

Chapter Fourteen:

Synergism

Synergism: The interaction of two or more agents or forces so that their combined effect is greater than the sum of their individual effects.

—The American Heritage Dictionary

From within the circle of my close associations I have watched a man grow from infancy to manhood. Even as an energetic, mischievous toddler it was clear that Rand was richly endowed with talent. By the time he graduated from high school we had seen that talent blossom. He was in the school choir, he played the lead in a couple of dramatic productions and he was on the track and football teams. All in all, he was a well-rounded, enthusiastic, optimistic teenager with a bright, promising future.

The next decade, however, was tough for Rand. He married at twenty-two, but the marriage didn't work out. Financial obligations incurred through his marriage and subsequent divorce prevented him from pursuing his education. He found himself struggling to make ends meet in a job he disliked. At thirty-two he was bitter, hurt, and cynical and beginning to believe that life would never again be as sweet and satisfying as it had been in high school.

Thankfully, Rand was unwilling to completely let go of his life-long dreams until he had made one last quest for fulfillment. So he began to rely on synergism by entering the graduate program he had wanted to pursue. Gradually, his dreams and vision for the future returned as he moved from the Mirrors stage in which he had been mired into the Windows stage. For the first time in years, he was hopeful for himself and the world in which he lived.

Of course, Julie had a lot to do with that. Julie was a young woman who came into Rand's life at about the same time he returned to college. She encouraged his educational dream and supported his decision to take charge of his life. With love, patience, and understanding she built his confidence in himself, and he in turn built hers. Together they created a synergism that was exciting to watch develop.

Today Rand and Julie are a dynamic, creative team moving forward together in their shared quest for a bright future of enthusiastic service and meaningful contribution. Together they are developing a power that is greater than the effect of the sum of their individual actions.

Or, in a word, synergism.

In a medical report dated March 20, 1992, a nationally noted internist reported the work of his study of synergism on various processes of the body. One aspect of the study was an examination of the response of endomorphines to a relaxation signal. At the heart of the study was the notion that our thoughts can influence these endomorphines and therefore dramatically influence the health of our system. This is a synergistic interaction: the combination of our thoughts interacting with our bodily responses to those thoughts creates a result that far exceeds the predicted combination of the two parts.

According to the report, people are healthier as they gain a sense of control over their lives. Inner peace and happiness help us cope with *all* of life's problems, including health. There is a completely synergistic relationship between Open Doors-type maturity and physical and mental health. And when we add the positive influence of those around us who are similarly at the Open Doors stage adding to that synergism, the potential for good is overwhelming.

The type of medicine discussed in the cited article is referred to as holistic medicine. It is based on the understanding that one bodily function influences another, and the whole system is dependent upon the interactions of one to the other. The point of holistic medicine is to strengthen the entire system by strengthening the interdependent parts.

I find it interesting that the words "whole" and "health" come from the same old English root word, "hal" as in "Hale and hearty." The synergistic relationship between "whole" and "health" is obvious. Our unhealthiness, according to this point of view, is in direct proportion to our inability to see it as a whole. If synergism is based on connectedness, holistic health is the synergistic connectedness of the mind and body.

Dr. Joan Borysenko, author of *Minding the Body, Mending the Mind,* is a pioneer in the field of holistic medicine. She is finding impressive results in the field of psychoneuroimmunology—the study of how the mind affects immunity. Dr. Borysenko indicates that there is much to illustrate the power of the mind in lowering blood pressure. Another finding has established the connectedness of stress to colds. The study also showed that our attitudes and beliefs have a significant impact on how we perceive stress. In other words, it is what goes on internally, not externally, that determines how we handle stress.

While I don't profess to be an expert on this subject, the notion of synergism between the body and the soul makes a great deal of sense to me. I know a young woman named Joan who has experienced a great deal of success in her thirty-one years. She has also known a great deal of health trouble. She seemed to be constantly dealing with colds, and she was developing symptoms of asthma and arthritis. Some nights as she tried to sleep she found it difficult to breath. And she lived with constant pain in her joints and muscles.

Doctors worked with her, but with no lasting impact. When she began to experience migraine headaches she went to her doctor in a panic. They talked for a long time about her lifestyle, her feelings, and her beliefs.

"I believe there is a connection between your style of life and your illness," the doctor said at last. "I would recommend you investigate some form of relaxation therapy. That is probably the best thing I can prescribe for you."

Joan did as her physician suggested. She learned some relaxation techniques including a form of meditation. She also began to ask herself, "Who am I?" and "What do I believe?" Her quest for meaning coupled with the relaxation techniques she was learning combined to her benefit.

One year later Joan went in for her physical examination and announced to her doctor: "I'm a new woman." Her quest for control over her inner-consciousness was having a positive impact on her body. She was a new woman physically, but she was also experiencing greater satisfaction and serenity in the mental and emotional aspects of her life.

Such synergism is a powerful concept in our lives. I have recently watched with great interest the synergistic exploits of a college basketball team. The team was picked to finish no higher than fourth in a nine-team athletic conference. They didn't have a single standout player. They had twelve players with good skills, but not a real star. It looked like a mediocre team that would experience a mediocre season.

But then the games began, and something interesting started happening. This group of athletes, all of them outstanding young people, became a team in the true sense of the word. They became each other's closest friends. They pulled together in practice and in games. They worked hard to help each other succeed, and discovered that in doing so, they all succeeded. One player would be the leading scorer in one game, the next game, another player would score the most. Sometimes the starting team would play the most minutes, and sometimes the reserves would take over for long stretches of time. Pretty soon it became clear that a synergistic relationship was emerging within this team.

That synergism was difficult for opposing teams to handle since many of those teams boasted more talent and brighter stars. The team won its conference, won its conference tournament and then went on to play respectably in the NCAA championship tournament. A team that was supposed to finish no higher than fourth flourished under the concept of synergism, which took them well beyond the predicted sum of their combined individual abilities. That resulted in symbiosis, with the entire team benefiting from the relationship despite their differences and abilities. That experience resulted in serendipity—an unforeseen, but delightful, consequence of both synergism and symbiosis, which we will discuss more thoroughly in the next chapter.

Research on team building—whether in the home, work place, or school—indicates that the key to a successful team is not the individual strength of each team member, but the connectedness of team members to each other and to the team itself. Senge uses Bill Russell's Boston Celtic professional basketball teams (winners of eleven NBA championships in thirteen years) to illustrate this synergistic relationship. He states: "this phenomenon [of the power of team-building] we have come to call 'alignment,' when a group of people function as a whole. In most teams, the energies of individual members work at cross purposes. If we draw a picture of a team as a collection of individuals with different degrees of 'personal power' [ability to accomplish results], headed different directions in their lives, we see a unit going in a variety of directions with this power. The fundamental characteristic of the relatively unaligned team is wasted energy."

By contrast, when a team becomes more aligned, a communality of direction emerges, and individual energies harmonize. There is less wasted energy. In fact, a resonance of synergy develops, like the coherent light of a laser, as opposed to the incoherent and scattered light of a light glove. This connectedness is the quality of synergism.

Builders know that one two-by-four standing on end will support 615 pounds. But two two-by-fours bound together will hold 2400 pounds, nearly four times more than what you would think two two-by-fours would logically support.

The same is true of people. Two people in a synergistic relationship have a combined strength well beyond the sum total of the capacity of each. And when you add more people to the synergism, you intensify their collective strength proportionally. Families, communities and businesses that create synergism through the quest for serendipity can achieve a synergistic energy of exciting individual and group magnitude.

The great moralist Aesop used to illustrate the concept this way: he would hold up a stick and ask for a volunteer among his listeners who thought they could break the stick. The volunteer was asked to come forward, and of course, was able to break the stick easily. Then Aesop would put two sticks of the same size together, and ask the same volunteer to break them both at the same time. It was more difficult, but usually it could be done without too much trouble. The process was repeated, with another stick added to the bundle each time, until the volunteer was unable to break the sticks. His moral: individually we are weak, but together we are strong.

Or, as Abraham Lincoln said, "United, we stand; divided, we fall."

Altruistic? Perhaps. But what's wrong with that?

Some years ago I was invited to appear before a state board of education to make a proposal for a major curriculum change. As I addressed the board, I sensed a positive response. Board members were asking good questions, and many heads were nodding affirmatively as I spoke of a plan built around the concepts of serendipity, synergism, and symbiosis. When I concluded my presentation, I was confident that my proposal would be accepted.

Later in the day I was asked to appear before the board again.

"Your proposal was clearly the most exciting and stimulating idea we have heard," the board president said. "However, as we considered it in light of the real problems and challenges we face working in the real world, we feel that it is too altruistic. Therefore, we must respectfully reject your plan."

I struggled with the rejection throughout my flight home.

"Too altruistic!" I thought. "How can a proposal to bring people together on a quest, to work hard, to not harm one another, to create strength beyond individual capacity be too altruistic?"

I decided that maybe I didn't understand what altruism is, so the next day I looked it up in my office dictionary. It defined altruism as "unselfishness, unselfish devotion to the interest and welfare of others, especially as a principle of action." Of altruistic it said, "being thoughtful of the welfare of others, unselfish."

Yes, I understood the meaning. And no, I decided I was not going to abandon my quest for these altruistic causes. For I truly believe that it is only through these efforts, labeled by some as "too altruistic," that the challenges of society can be overcome.

Remember Rand and Julie? As they came together in their quest for authenticity, they united synergistically to bring others around them together in common causes to make their community a better place. Not only did they strengthen each other, but they brought friendship and service to the neighborhood, and influenced many others to join them on their quest.

As a result, this neighborhood influenced the entire community in which it was located. Through the efforts of Rand and Julie and their neighbors, the community became more mindful of the hungry and homeless. They helped integrate minorities into the community and developed scholarships and jobs to help people become more self-reliant. They helped to create an environment that brought individuals and groups out of the circumstances that had them trapped—by developing vision, hope, and dreams. Because of the synergistic efforts of Rand and Julie many people learned to bring *who they are* and *what they do* into harmony, thus becoming *authentic* people themselves.

Such good within the individual, the family, the community, and the work place is beautiful to contemplate. Life would be sweeter.

Society would be more compassionate. And the world would be a more wonderful place if we could all reach down and bring the inner power of these principles to the surface in our own lives and in the lives of those around us.

Of course, this can only happen as we come to know ourselves and our connectedness with others well enough to trust and develop faith in self, others and a power or cause greater than self. When we can do this we become *authentic* people. Our lives are simplified as we create for ourselves and others the peace and serenity that comes with authenticity—synergistically and serendipitously.

The Hall family was experiencing a tragedy of great proportions. Amy, one of their three children, had run away. She had been gone for three days when they decided to call the police. An officer came to their home to gather information on Amy—photographs, friends' names, relationships, and such. As the family shared their insights and feelings about Amy, a divisive tone began to emerge.

"If you hadn't been so mean to her, she wouldn't have left," one family member said to another.

"All you ever did was tease her," another family member replied. "You were always hassling her about the size of her nose."

"She didn't mind that," the family member said. "What bugged her is the way Dad used to ride her."

"Well," the father said, "if she hadn't been so stubborn and disobedient I wouldn't have had to be on her back all the time."

After several heated moments of this back-and-forth blaming, a heavy silence fell over the room. At last, the police officer asked quietly: "Is your family like this all the time?"

The family members looked at each other. "Not all the time," the mother said.

"Most of the time?" the officer asked.

"It's like this a lot," the father acknowledged.

The officer shrugged. "Maybe that had something to do with Amy running away," he said. "I know I wouldn't want to live in a house where it felt like this house feels right now."

I'm pleased to be able to report that some good came out of this experience. Amy called a couple of days later from an aunt's house in a neighboring state. She was safe and healthy, but she insisted that she would not return to the type of home life she left behind. While she said she loved her family, she hated the feelings she felt in her home through criticism, sarcasm, and conflict. Eventually, the desire to get away from those feelings overwhelmed her, and she ran away.

And she said she wouldn't come back unless things could be significantly changed.

It was agreed that Amy would stay with her aunt while the family became involved with family counseling. During the next year the family gained individual and collective strength through looking within themselves and working together to connect with each other. Amy also received help through counseling, and gained strength and inner-confidence that she had never possessed. When at last she returned to her home, the family began the laborious process of re-connecting—one-by-one.

Synergy has helped the Hall family to heal. Out of chaos, they have created an inner-strength to deal with the ambiguities of life without turning on each other. They have been able to eliminate the need to manipulate their external environment and have achieved a more *authentic* lifestyle. They have also discovered that even when external chaos threatens to complicate their lives, the strength they have gained individually—and the synergistic strength they have gained collectively—gives them the ability to remain cohesively and coherently unified.

Such synergism is dependent upon individuals in a process of growth. As individuals grow, they are better able to serve others and help them grow. As each individual in the Hall family gained control over their inner-consciousness, they were able to create familial synergy that is bringing positive results in their lives, individually and collectively. Others are also helped as they see a practical working model of how the Hall's have worked through adversity to create a synergistic relationship of hope and growth.

The Scandinavian tale of "The Sheep and the Pig," re-told in William J. Bennett's *Book of Virtues*, teaches this principle:

> One morning, bright and early, a sheep and a curly-tailed pig started out through the world to find a home.
>
> "We will build us a house," said the sheep and the curly-tailed pig, "and there we will live together."
>
> So they went a long, long way until they came to a rabbit.
>
> "Where are you going?" the rabbit asked.
>
> "We are going to build us a house," said the sheep and pig.
>
> "May I live with you?" asked the rabbit.

"What can you do to help?" asked the sheep and pig.

The rabbit said: "I can gnaw pegs with my sharp teeth; I can put them in with my paws."

"Good!" said the sheep and the pig. "You may come with us."

So the three went on a long, long way further until they came to a gray goose.

"Where are you going?" asked the gray goose.

"We are going to build us a house," said the sheep, the pig and the rabbit.

"May I live with you?" asked the gray goose.

"What can you do to help?" asked the sheep, the pig and the rabbit.

The gray goose said: "I can pull moss and stuff it in the cracks with my broad bill."

"Good!" said the sheep, the pig, and the rabbit. "You may come with us."

So the four went along a long, long way until they came to a barnyard rooster.

"Where are you going?" asked the rooster of the four.

"We are going to build us a house," said the sheep, the pig, the rabbit, and the goose.

"May I live with you?" asked the rooster.

"What can you do to help?" asked the sheep, the pig, the rabbit, and the goose.

The rooster said: "I can crow very early every morning; I can awaken you all."

"Good!" said the sheep, the pig, the rabbit, and the goose. "You may come with us."

So the five went on a long, long way until they found a good place for a house.

Then the sheep hewed logs and drew them.

The pig made bricks for the cellar.

The rabbit gnawed pegs with his sharp teeth, and hammered them in with his paws.

The goose pulled moss and stuffed it in the cracks with her bill.

The rooster crowed early every morning to tell them that it was time to rise.

And they all lived happily together in their little house.

System theory in organizational behavior uses a principle of nature, which seems to have learned to design in pairs. Two legs are necessary for rapid, flexible locomotion. Two arms and hands are critical for climbing, lifting and manipulating objects. Two eyes give us stereoscopic vision and depth perception. And, as we have noted previously, two types of vision are required to create the complete life perspective we call "whole sight."

When the mind's eye and the soul connect, authentic spirituality opens us to truth. Such spirituality encourages us to welcome diversity, to reject conflict, to tolerate ambiguity and to embrace paradox. The "whole sight" of the mind's eye and the soul creates a synergism that will drive out fear, which gives ignorance its power. It will ground us in the confidence of our search for truth—and truth's search for us. This brings us another step closer to full authenticity, and a relationship of trust between self and others.

Chapter Fifteen:

Symbiosis

Symbiosis: The living together in more or less intimate association or close union of two dissimilar organisms; the intimate living together of two dissimilar organisms in a mutually beneficial relationship; a cooperative relationship (as between two persons or groups).

—*Websters Ninth New Collegiate Dictionary*

Although some scientists might disagree, it seems to me that few organisms are as dissimilar from each other as one human being is from another. While it's true we may be similar to each other in many ways, each one of us is different biologically, physically, emotionally, psychologically and socially. But I believe that as we mature to the Open doors stage of living, the serendipity principle allows for all of this work that we've been doing to come together symbiotically, for the benefit of all, despite our deepest differences.

That means husbands and wives can live together symbiotically, where both partners benefit from the intensely intimate relationship *despite*—or maybe even *because of*—their differences. The work place can be a nurturing haven of sensitivity, caring, cooperation, and peace and entire communities can come together in a spirit of harmony and love if differences between people are down-played and mutual benefits are stressed—symbiotically, synergistically, serendipitously, and otherwise.

Bob and Andrea felt an immediate attraction to each other when they were introduced at work. Despite reservations each had about dating someone from the office, they soon began courting, and three months later they were married.

Their courtship had been delightful. They found so many things that they had in common, from their mutual love for silent movies to their shared disdain for country music. Within days after they were married, however, the similarities began giving way to cavernous differences. Andrea was a high school graduate; Bob had an MBA from Stanford. Andrea was a conservative, fundamental Christian; Bob was agnostic. Andrea came from a blue collar, midwestern family; Bob's parents were both successful Southern California professionals. Andrea came from a home with a strong, patriarchal father figure; Bob came from a home with a dominating, almost domineering mother.

Talk about dissimilar organisms! Andrea read the Bible and prayed every night; Bob declined her invitations to join in her devotionals because he didn't value participation. Andrea wanted five or six children right away; Bob wasn't sure he wanted any—ever. Andrea wanted to quit her job and be a full-time homemaker; Bob thought she should continue working outside the home so they could afford to hire people to do all of the household chores for them.

Faced with such a wide disparity in backgrounds and values, many people would be inclined to write off the marriage as an unfortunate mistake. But Bob and Andrea were bound by a powerful love that allowed them to cling to the belief that they could experience and enjoy a completely symbiotic relationship if they were just willing to work hard enough to make it happen.

It wasn't easy. It took time, patience, and sensitivity to wade through the mine fields of their respective differences looking for symbiosis. But they knew and understood that they, and they alone, controlled their mutual destiny, and they took meaningful responsibility for the outcome of their relationship.

They began by setting aside time to talk. They shared their thoughts and values with each other, not as a way of proselyting or trying to convince the other that one perspective is superior to another, but simply as a way of learning, growing, and understanding. They analyzed why they behaved the way they did in given circumstances. They took a good, long look at themselves in the mirrors of *who others think I am, who I see myself becoming, and who I am.* They developed windows of shared hope, dreams, and vision, and opened doors to becoming *authentic* people—together.

They established an ongoing process of working toward their shared quest of authenticity (serendipity), and participated constantly in a process of bringing their dissimilar mental models together in an attempt to connect with common values (symbiosis).

Does that sound too complicated? Then let's put it this way: Because they were committed to each other and to their relationship, they learned how to down-play their differences and accentuate their shared virtues in ways that were mutually beneficial and satisfying.

In other words, they achieved symbiosis.

Now, take the story of Andrea and Bob and multiply it by all of the families, neighborhoods, businesses, and communities that could benefit from such interpersonal symbiosis. Can you see the potential far-reaching value of following the principles of becoming an *authentic* person? The world does not succeed on the basis of separate, unrelated forces. Institutions, from marriage to the federal government, can only flourish with the healthy, creative process of interaction one with another. And symbiotic relationships can only develop among people who have a pretty good fix on *who they are* and who understand *who they are becoming.*

Growth in any organization begins with individual growth. As individuals learn to meet and overcome challenges and obstacles, they develop significant skills that can be shared with others in the organization. When those individuals are blended with others who have reached similar levels of maturity, there is enhanced potential for symbiotic relationships that can benefit all of the individuals within the organization as well as the organization itself.

The process of symbiosis creates faith. For our purposes here, we will define faith as a set of beliefs or virtues that permeate an entire organization, giving it a spiritual center of meaning and giving its members a sense of purpose and shared covenants; it is those shared covenants that draw together the creative forces necessary for real growth through symbiosis.

In order to create such a symbiosis within a group; however, it is important that each individual member of the group feel included and important. At one time or another we've all experienced the feeling of being left out of a group, or not being included. I remember being in just such a situation early in my college days. I was at a social function, and I was overwhelmed and intimidated by the group. I observed for a while, hoping to be included but never making any effort at including myself. I finally decided that I was totally inadequate to the situation and was about to leave when a professor stopped me.

"You're not going to leave, are you?" he asked.

"Well, yes," I said, hesitantly. "I don't seem to be accomplishing anything here."

"Of course you aren't," he said. "But it isn't because you don't belong. It's because you aren't trying."

"I'm not sure I . . ."

"Look, you're waiting for them to include you in the group, aren't you?" Reluctantly, I agreed. "And they're waiting for you to work your way in. So everyone is waiting, and nothing is happening."

He was right about that. No question about it.

"What it comes down to is this," the professor continued. "We all have to work to expand what Einstein called 'our circle of compassion.' You need the group, and the group needs you. But the only way it's going to happen is if you extend yourself and jump in."

So I did. It wasn't easy, and I felt a little uncomfortable. But it worked, and by the end of the evening the group was important to me and I was important to the group.

That's how it works in a symbiotic relationship: the success of the whole is dependent upon the success of each individual part. It's sort of like my lawn. One year my yard didn't look very well, and I couldn't figure out what the problem was. I fertilized it. I watered it more. I watered it less. Nothing worked. At last I brought in a lawn specialist to take a look at it.

"Earth worms," she pronounced after a quick tour of the yard.

I was stunned. I hadn't seen a worm all season. "I have earth worms?" I asked.

"No," she said patiently. "You *don't* have them. That's the problem. Somehow you've killed all of the earthworms in your yard."

"And that's bad?"

"Sure is. Worms aerate the soil. Some folks call 'em 'God's little plows.' Without them in there moving the earth around, your soil has compacted. That's why the roots of your lawn are having such a hard time getting any nutrients. It's tough on roots without earth worms down there loosening things up."

Similarly, each one of us individually contribute to the whole of our physical, social, and spiritual environment. Throughout this book we have talked about individual growth toward authenticity. This is an important and necessary process. But to create a great marriage, family, neighborhood, community, or business, we must learn how to develop shared vision. Authenticity has the potential for more power in a group setting than it does in our respective individual quests. In fact, groups that learn to create relationships of trust, develop common mental models and work together toward these common visions often create more powerful outcomes than anything an individual can create, regardless of their authenticity.

Recently I attended a conference conducted by a noted child psychologist. One of her main points was that the neighborhood has as much influence on teen behavior as the home. She spoke about the effect of these environments on children in their most formative years.

During the question and answer period a woman asked her what she would look for in moving with her children to a new neighborhood. The woman indicated her family was making a move, and she was concerned for her two children.

The speaker's answer was very specific.

"If I had children at home," she said, "I would never buy a new house until I had gone door-to-door in the neighborhood to talk to people to find out what kind of relationships exist in the area. Do the people who live here have close relationships? What kind of shared values are in existence?

"Basically," she continued, "I would try to see what symbiotic relationships exist in the neighborhood and community."

She went on to say that she and her husband chose their current home based on these mental models rather than on the house itself.

"The house has not been our dream home," she said, "but the neighborhood has been our dream neighborhood. We have important shared values that have helped us all through some difficult times. The families in the neighborhood are a great team and true friends. We don't just live together; we laugh together, we cry together, we play together, and we work together. And we have found that as our children have gone off on their own they search for neighborhoods and groups with this same spirit of symbiosis."

This process can only occur among individuals and groups who are able to get outside of themselves, who see in others opportunities to serve, who are in the process of creating environments where others can grow through nurturing and service. When you live among people who share your values, and who allow those values to drive the choices they make for the common good—choices that are directed toward fulfilling shared covenants—you begin to understand the powerful positive influence of symbiosis in our lives and in the lives of those who we love—differences notwithstanding.

As we achieve a state of symbiosis in our lives, we begin to realize that our environment or culture completes us as humans. Culture is not indigenous clothing that covers the universal human. It infuses individuals, fundamentally shaping and forming us and how we interpret ourselves and our place in the world around us. Through it we come to understand how we should view others, how we should engage in structures of mutual obligation and how we make choices every day of our lives.

If relationships consist of two or more "empty self" individuals, then the culture they create will be an "empty self" culture, devoid of community, tradition, and shared values. If, on the other hand, relationships are built by two or more people who are working toward filling the "empty self" with an inner core of virtues, the culture they create will be one with a greater opportunity to develop a sense of community, tradition, and shared values.

By basing *what we do* on a true *who we are* foundation, we create an *authentic* community, an *authentic* tradition, and an *authentic* shared value underpinning. Far too many times our efforts to create these qualities are only faddish and shallow. We must remember that it all starts with one person who is willing to enter into a quest (serendipity) and connect with others on a quest (synergism) to enter into symbiotic relationships built on community, tradition, and shared values.

There's an old popular song that says, "Give me some men who are stout-hearted men and I'll soon give you ten thousand more." This is the process of symbiosis. We do not live alone; "no man is an island." We must enter into *authentic* symbiotic relationships for true happiness to prevail.

Let me describe a real-life neighborhood that achieved these qualities as well as any I have ever observed. At the time it was an upper-middle class neighborhood, a new housing development of about thirty homes. Almost every family that bought or built homes in the area came from distant locations, which gave the neighborhood an interesting mix of people from a variety of backgrounds and livelihoods.

As the homes were finished and people moved in, friendships began to develop among immediate neighbors. But for one man in the neighborhood, that wasn't enough. And thanks largely to his efforts, a broader sense of symbiotic community was cultivated.

He launched his campaign innocently enough. Whenever a family was working on their rocky yard, raking off the rocks and hauling them away, this neighbor would show up with a rake and a wheelbarrow to work shoulder-to-shoulder with his new neighbor. His example was contagious and soon there was an extensive network of neighbors helping neighbors with putting in yards and sprinkling systems. A general feeling of "connectedness" began to develop.

During these times of working together, a conversation developed. Individuals gradually melted into a community where everyone felt as if they belonged. As the conversation continued through working together, through neighborhood dinners, through community classes, and through music recitals and little league ball games, a shared intrinsic vision began to emerge.

It became obvious as the conversation continued through time that they were all concerned about rearing their families with an inner core of virtues to guide their lives. They also shared the sense of belonging, of continuity, of connectedness to others, and to ideas and virtues that make life meaningful and significant. As time went on, a shared vision developed of what life could be like.

As a result of this neighborhood-wide connectedness, the children in the area didn't seek new identity in external satisfactions. They were unified, and an attached, cooperative, trusting friendship developed among them. They played together, cried together, dated each other, and enjoyed growth in a culture of vision and virtue.

As adversity came into individual families, an automatic support system swung into gear. As problems became more complex, the community grew ever tighter and more unified. Together they focused on lifting aspirations, often asking themselves, "What do we want to create here?" The unified answer to this question created a mental model of Utopia in each neighbor's mind.

The modeling of this lifestyle has caused several of the now-married children from the community to come back and ask, "Where do we find a neighborhood like this one?"

The answer: "You don't find it, you create it. This neighborhood was not like this when we moved in. We had to create it by developing a shared vision of the virtues that guide our behavior."

A vitality existed in that neighborhood as their individual creative influence took on the form of a quest, uniting with others in a shared quest guided by the question, "What do we want to create?"

The next question is, "How do we do it?"

The answer: "You gotta wanna." You have to really want something to happen before anything actually will happen. One person willing to enter into a quest can create a serendipitous process that creates a connectedness or synergism, which in turn creates a symbiotic relationship in the family, the neighborhood, the community, the church, and the nation. It all starts with one, and the one can easily be you or me.

Too altruistic? Too idealistic? A good idea, but it won't work in your neighborhood, or your family? That's up to you. The space will be filled and the culture will be created, either by your efforts or by the natural external forces that are always there to fill the empty space.

Louise was riding the bus home after a long day's work. The bus was crowded, and she was standing in the aisle, holding on to the bar above her. She began to feel as if she couldn't breathe, but not just because the bus was crowded. It was more like emotional claustrophobia. As she stood there being jostled by the crowd and jolted by the movement of the bus, her mind went to her last fishing trip with her family. They had camped in a beautiful open meadow, with a clear mountain stream running through it. As she bounced along on her bus ride, she contrasted what she was feeling right then to what she had felt in that meadow. In the meadow she had felt open to thoughts, ideas, and feelings. She had experienced a creativity she hadn't felt in her day-to-day environment. She felt as if her knowledge was coming out of hiding. But on the bus, she felt as if she couldn't even think.

As she continued to consider what she was feeling, she reflected on her daily work. Most days she felt pressed and crowded. She didn't have space because of the urgency of deadlines and the competitiveness of her colleagues. But on the days when deadlines disappeared and colleagues cooperated, when everyone had the space to move, invent, and produce with energy and enthusiasm, life at work was more like life in that meadow—well, at least a little.

Of course, there were also times when that same claustrophobic feeling permeated her life at home and in her neighborhood, particularly when family members and friends placed what she felt were unreasonable demands on her. The constant expectations crowded her in. She didn't have "space," just like on the bus.

The concept of "space" is real in our lives—physically, mentally, and spiritually—and we have all experienced occasional bouts of claustrophobia. These are the times when you feel trapped, as if you are being controlled and your "space" is filled with external influences. Most of us instinctively resist such enclosure, although many of us learn to accept and deal with it as a natural part of our lives.

But there is a way to eliminate this condition from our lives, and it is by following the mental model we have outlined on the preceding pages. Ultimately, the way to open "space" and fill it with self-determined goals and virtues, must be through entering into symbiotic relationships. Only through our personal growth connected to others will symbiosis eliminate claustrophobia in our lives. And only through shared virtues in symbiotic relationships can trust be created and find a common identity with which to create truth.

Symbiotic relationships grow from "whole sight," the mind's eye and the soul united. Any organization can grow when imbued with "whole sight" direction based on sensitivity, serenity, support, belongingness, and openness. Shared "whole sight" is an exciting concept to contemplate.

In *Credibility*, James McKouzes and Berry Posner illustrate this important concept with the following story:

> Once there was a village in Nigeria, West Africa, where the people made their living by farming. The village lay in a large green valley that was lined with palm trees and bushes. Surrounding the village were fields dotted with crops of yams, cassava, corn and other vegetables. Just beyond the fields was a deep river that the villagers called Bab, which means father. The river was a friend and a provider for the people: the men used it for fishing, the women washed clothes on its banks and the children played in its waters. But in the rainy season, the river overflowed, and the people were fearful of its power. So, at a place where the river wound beyond the fields, they built a strong dam to hold back the water.
>
> There was a man in the village named Modupe, which means "I am grateful." Modupe was a shy, quiet man whose wife had died and whose children were all married, so he had moved to the top of the mountain overlooking the valley and lived alone. There he had built a small hut and cleared a small piece of land to grow his vegetables. The people did

not see Modupe often, but they loved and respected him because he had the gift of healing the sick and because he was one of them.

One year at harvest time, there were unusually heavy rains, but the crops had done well and there was much to do. No one paid it any mind. As Modupe stood by his house on the mountain, he noticed that the river had become swollen from the rains and was straining the dam. He knew that by the time he could run down to the village to warn the people of the flood, it would be too late and all would be lost. Even as Modupe watched, the wall of the dam began to break, and water started to seep through.

Modupe thought of his friends in the village. Their crops, their homes and their very lives were in danger if he did not find a way to warn them. Then an idea came to him: he rushed to his small hut and set it afire. When the people of the valley saw Modupe's house burning, they said, "Our friend is in trouble. Let's sound the alarm and go up to help him." Then, according to custom, men, women, and children ran up the mountain to see what they could do. When they reached the top of the hill, they did not have time to ask what had happened—a loud crashing noise behind them made them turn around and look down into the valley. Their houses, their temple, and their crops were being destroyed by the river, which had broken the dam and was flooding the valley.

The people began to cry and moan at their loss, but Modupe comforted them. "Don't worry," he said. "My crops are still here. We can share them while we build a new village." Then all the people began to sing and give thanks because they remembered that in coming to help a friend, they had saved themselves.

Shelley Brown of Aspect Telecommunication says that "shared values are the glue that holds this organization together." Coming together through shared virtues, building relationships of trust and having shared values doesn't necessarily mean that everyone within the organization or community believes in the same things or agrees on every issue. It just means that they have a common covenant on truth, gratitude, charity, self-discipline and courage as virtues guiding behavior. These shared virtues would be the building blocks of productive and genuine relationships—differences notwithstanding. Diversity could still be recognized and encouraged, but the conversation would be built on truth, expressing and feeling gratitude, with charity directing all behavior. Self-discipline would be the constant control of discussion, and the courage to hold to basic convictions would dominate every thought and action.

When shared virtues are recognized, the conversation is driven by a common language, generating tremendous energy. With these shared virtues, groups can be more creative. The connection between common vision and virtues is empowering to all concerned.

The process of arriving at symbiosis is well-expressed in Myra Brooks Welch's wonderful poem, "The Touch of the Master's Hand":

Twas battered and scarred, and the auctioneer
Thought it scarcely worth his while
To waste his time on the old violin,
But he held it up with a smile.

"What am I bid, good friends," said he.
"Who'll start the bidding for me?
One dollar? Only one? Who'll make it two?
Two dollars? And who'll make it three?

"Three dollars once, and three dollars twice,
And going and going . . ." But no.
From the back of the room a gray-haired man
Came forward and picked up the bow.

And wiping the dust from the old violin
And tightening the loose strings
He played a melody pure and sweet
As caroling angels sing.

The music ceased, and the auctioneer
In a voice that was quiet and low
Said, "What am I bid for the old violin?"
As he held it up with the bow.

"One thousand dollars? And who'll make it two?
Two thousand? And who'll make it three?
"Three thousand once, and three thousand twice,
And going and going and gone!" said he.

The crowd cheered! But some of them cried
"We do not quite understand
What changed its worth." Swift came the reply:
"'Twas the touch of the master's hand."

The instrument can make the sound, but it takes the master to turn the sound into music. The bonding of the violin and the master created a synergism of power, increasing the value of the instrument many fold.

And so it is with us. As we join our mind's eye and our soul we greatly increase our value to ourselves and to the world around us. We create a synergistic strength beyond our individual worth—just as was the case with the old violin. And as the violin and its master join forces with the diversity of other mastered instruments that make up the individual parts of an orchestra, we have a symbiotic potential through harmony that can be extraordinary—almost miraculous. Enter another master with the talent and mental images of the potential of the various parts, and the result can be a symphony of beauty that lifts the souls of listeners and performers to higher heights.

Welch concludes her poem with these thought-provoking verses:

And many a man with life out of tune
And battered and scarred with sin
Is auctioned cheap to the thoughtless crowd
Much like the old violin.

A mess of pottage, a glass of wine,
A game and he travels on.
He's going once, and going twice,
And going and almost gone.

'Til the master comes, and the thoughtless crowd
Never can quite understand
The worth of a soul and the change that is wrought
By the touch of the master's hand.

Many have been willing to enter this quest of discovering *who we are* and have worked to bring that notion into harmony with *what we do* by directing thoughts and intrinsic virtues. As a result, they have become masters of their own "self." In so doing, they have been able to overcome fear and therefore gain faith. They have united their mind's eye with their soul to master truth, gratitude, charity, self-discipline, and courage.

When we master ourselves, we are immune to criticism and easily bonded to others. Because we don't struggle for approval and don't feel a need to control anyone else, this bonding can come from the heart and the soul. Therefore a synergy occurs that places us in a space of being a creative power.

As we form these bonds, our relationships with others expand. Our bonded strengths expand our potential for influence as we experience the serenity and beauty of serving others through the unity of our mind's eye and soul. Symbiotic relationships fill the spaces of our lives. The music of our mastery over the various instruments of life now makes it possible to be a part of a symphony of bonded relationships. In this symphony we give our life to a power greater than ourself and allow the Master to orchestrate our service to mankind through the unity of *who we are* and *what we do*.

Epilogue:

When Mind and Heart Unite

Many of us live one-eyed lives. We rely largely on the eye of the mind to form our image of reality. But today more and more of us are opening the other eye the eye of the heart—looking for realities to which the mind's eye is blind. Either eye alone is not enough. We need "whole sight," a vision of the world in which mind and heart unite.

—Parker J. Palmer

I'm a morning person. Always have been. Probably always will be. I think it's one of the hazards of growing up on a farm. As far as I'm concerned, there's just no better time of the day than those early morning hours when the peaceful quiet of the night is illuminated by the dawn's gentle light. Often I will spend those precious moments in our living room reading and thinking as a way of preparing myself for the rigors of the day ahead.

One morning as I was browsing through a series of thoughts my eyes came to rest on a violet that had been planted in a pot and positioned on our fireplace hearth. I had seen this particular violet dozens of times, but for some reason I hadn't noticed how sick-looking and frail it had become. There were no blossoms and only a few small leaves, and the entire plant drooped feebly.

"Poor thing," I thought as I carried the pot toward the trash. "Violets are such beautiful flowers. If only we had taken better care of this one." I smiled as I caught myself in the *if only* trap, and I forced myself to think in terms of "what if . . . ?"

"What if I take this little plant and do everything I can to nurse it back to health?" I asked. "I wonder what it can become."

So I decided to try. Later that morning, I hopped in the car and drove to a nearby nursery, where I picked up a little booklet on violets. I studied it carefully and began to follow its instructions for raising healthy, beautiful violets.

The first step was to transplant the flower into a larger container, so the roots would have adequate room for growth. Then I went back to the nursery to pick up some rich potting soil that was conducive to plant nourishment. I also learned from that little booklet that my violet would do best in indirect western light and that water needed to be applied in just the right amounts at just the right time. Even the kind and volume of fertilizer was specified, and I followed those instructions carefully.

Within a few weeks I began to see a difference in my droopy little violet. Within a few months, the plant was flourishing. It had beautiful blossoms and large, healthy leaves. I was proud of what I had accomplished, and grateful that I had taken the time to ask "what if...?"

Unfortunately, the story doesn't end there. One evening some friends came to visit with their five small—and very active— children. We were chatting in the living room when I happened to glance out the window and notice a glorious sunset on the western horizon. I suggested that we continue our conversation on the front porch, where we could all enjoy the sunset while we talked. The adults adjourned outside while the children remained in the living room—alone—with my violet.

That's right—you guessed it. By the time we returned to the living room my violet was a limp pile of torn blossoms and shredded leaves. The children didn't mean any harm, but in just a few unattended minutes they had destroyed what had taken me months to create.

We have been discussing at length the steps you must travel on your personal journey toward an *authentic* life. It is likely that it will require considerable time and effort on your part to move through the steps of Mirrors, Windows, and Open Doors as you create the style of living that you want for yourself. Indeed, the creative process never ends, for our lives are constantly changing and evolving, requiring adjustments and alterations all along the way. Even when you arrive at your desired state of authentism, you will discover that it is as fragile and delicate as . . . well, my violet. And just as my violet could be destroyed in a few intense, undisciplined moments, so too could all of the work you do toward creating an *authentic* life for yourself disappear under a thoughtless flood of pride, anger, bitterness, or fear.

This is a marvelous journey upon which you are embarking. But it is also fraught with peril. Life is pretty simple in the Mirrors stage, where external influences do all of your thinking for you. As you move into the Windows stage and become more aware of yourself and others and the world in which we all live, you increase the possibility of happiness and joy as well as the possibility of pain and disappointment. The heightened sensitivity of the Open Doors stage also means heightened vulnerability. Reaching out to others with love and understanding exposes us to both the possibility of being embraced or getting our face slapped.

Which means that there is risk involved in this process, as there is with almost anything worthwhile. I submit to you that the potential rewards of an *authentic* life far outweigh any possible difficulties, and that the risk is worth it. But you'll have to make that decision for yourself. If you do decide to make the journey, I urge you to do so with caution and care. Make sure that your hopes, dreams, and visions are tenderly nurtured and well protected. Cultivate meaningful relationships with people who are capable of caring about you as much as you care about them. Avoid harsh, destructive behaviors that can sap positive energy, drain health, and damage lives.

Above all else, keep the path that links your mind with your heart clear and uncluttered that you might have the "whole sight" Parker J. Palmer spoke of in the quotation cited a few pages ago. For it is only as mind and heart unite that we can both know and understand the importance of our individual life well-lived. We can study its reflection in other people's mirrors and we can see it for ourselves through the windows of our own soul. But until we strip ourselves of narcissism and step through open doors to experience first-hand the joyful exhilaration of giving, caring, serving and loving others selflessly, we will never fully know what it is to be a whole, complete, *authentic* person.

So what are you waiting for? Go ahead and take that risk! Your journey inward toward becoming an *authentic* person awaits! And don't be surprised if you discover that the reward lies not so much in arriving at your destination, but in the journey itself.

Helpful
Exercises
to Guide Our
Journey

Exercise One

Would you like to know how you're doing in making your way through the mirrors, windows, and open doors of your life? A detailed diary has always been an effective tool for evaluating personal progress and growth.

Wait just a minute! Before you completely tune me out, please let me explain. I'm not asking you to commit to keep a diary for the rest of your life (although I must admit, it wouldn't be a bad thing if you did). I'm only suggesting that you try it for one day. But you must be very committed to the project for that one day or else it will never accomplish what we hope to achieve.

Here's what you do: find a small notebook that you can fit in your pocket or purse. From the time you get up in the morning, take a minute or two at the end of each hour to record transpired events as well as your thoughts and feelings about them. Your record doesn't need to be long, but it should be accurate and precise. At the end of the day you will summarize your record and develop conclusions and goals.

It should go something like this:

10-11 a.m.

Event:

Continued attendance at staff meeting until 10:30 a.m. Returned to office. Returned five phone calls. Provided directions and instructions to three employees.

Thoughts:

I was not given an opportunity to comment on an important issue, and I decided not to assert myself. I should have. The phone calls and people who needed me to talk to them all required someone else's approval or direction to do their work. Interesting how dependent we all are upon others in this organization. Is it like this everywhere?

Feelings:

> *All I do is what someone else tells me to do. I can see areas where I could improve both myself and others, but that's not the way it works around here. It's frustrating. I wish I could provide more input for some creative solutions.*

At the end of the day you'll have about fifteen similar entries providing a detailed account of your day from the beginning to the end. Now it's time to summarize, taking into account your personal responsibility (which responsibilities you accept, avoid, ignore, neglect, want, need, and so forth), your time (how you use it and abuse it), and the thoughts you had when you didn't have to think (where your thoughts went when you didn't have to focus them for a specific purpose). For example:

Personal Responsibility

> *I think my frustration and modest level of motivation in life come from the fact that I feel trapped by the circumstances of my life. I am not creating my life; it's being created for me. More than eighty percent of my day was spent responding to someone else's expectations without regard to my own sense of what should be done.*

Time

> *As I analyze my day I realize I have been involved in a variety of quick-fix type activities with very little thought of the long term. I don't have time to really solve my own problems, let alone the problems of others in the department. All I do is provide band-aid solutions. I realize that all my activities are controlled by past traditions and ways of doing things. There's no time, or I don't take the time, to think about the future. I find myself becoming more and more resentful of how I spend my time.*

Thoughts I Had When I Didn't Have to Think

> *My summary of this section worries me. My thoughts are shallow and not very productive or positive. I often think about getting out and away from my present life. I don't think I had one uplifting thought about myself, my work, or my relationships with others today.*

Now that you've summarized and analyzed your day, develop two or three goals to enhance your personal satisfaction, progress, or happiness. Given the example diary and analysis above, you might wish to set goals that would help you exert more positive influence on your environment, take more initiative in creating your own destiny, or create more stimulating activities in your daily life. Remember to make your specific; don't just say "I will begin exerting more positive influence on my environment," but indicate some specific things you will do to make that happen. And make sure your goals will really achieve the desired result. After all, you don't want to expend a lot of energy scaling a peak only to find out after you're there that you've climbed the wrong mountain.

Remember, I have only suggested that you keep a detailed diary for one day. But I should mention that additional days will provide additional insights. Once you think you have a pretty good idea of where you are on your journey to becoming an authentic person you're ready to begin reading the next section about turning mirrors into windows of understanding and opportunity.

Exercise Two

Before we move into the Open Door stage of our process of becoming an *authentic* person, let's do a little more mirroring. At the end of Section One you recorded a diary of at least one day's worth of activities. You analyzed your activities from the standpoint of how your use of time and your behavior resulted from external expectations.

Now we're going to go back to that diary and record an additional three days worth of thoughts and feelings. Follow the same pattern of recording and analyzing. This time, however, we will factor in a few additional aspects of our recorded life:

1. Continue to analyze how much of your behavior is directed toward satisfying others' expectations. Is it less now, more or the same as the first day's record?

2. Now add the dimension of how much of your time is influenced by who I think I can become. Identify those thoughts—particularly when you don't have to think—that take you outside yourself to serving other people and outside causes in the family, neighborhood, and community.

3. Determine what you are actually doing to develop a core of personal values that will strengthen your commitment to the things you really believe in.

For example:

9-10 a.m.

Event:

Met with employee who is not performing his work duties satisfactorily. We spoke for an hour. I asked my secretary to hold all calls while I met with Jim.

Thoughts:

My inclination was to apply long-standing company rules and policies to Jim's behavior. But I decided to first explore to see if I could find reasons why Jim was missing so much work and performing so poorly when he is here. Jim was surprised I even cared.

He said it was the first time anyone seemed more interested in him than in what he did for the company. He poured out his heart about feelings of inadequacy, lack of direction. He described some health problems in his family that were causing financial and emotional strain at home. I really feel like we know each other better now.

Feelings:

It would have been easy to slip back into patterns of allowing regulation to govern behavior. I had to keep reminding myself to focus on people instead of policy. But I think this is a superior approach. I felt good after our meeting. I'm sure Jim did, too.

At the end of each day you'll have fifteen sets of entries similar to the one above. Now you can summarize each day's events and feelings in terms of the following:

- Is my behavior based more on internal values or external influences? What events support that conclusion?

- Am I taking time to find long-term solutions to problems, or am I resorting to quick-fixes? What events support that conclusion?

- What did I think about when I didn't have to think? Are my thoughts getting outside of myself and focusing on other people and causes? What thoughts support that conclusion?

Write this analysis at the end of each of the three days you monitor. Based on the trends you see through your analysis, set two goals that will help you bring *who you are* and *what you do* into closer harmony.

Exercise Three

We are now ready to take another look at ourselves. You have read the major points of this compass, which is intended to guide your path to the North Star of authenticity. We have discussed the process of creating our own destiny by developing mental models.

Mental models are changed by experience. Experiences are directed through the thoughts we allow to stay in our mind. The process of choosing thoughts is the process of valuing. What we value, we do.

Those processes are ongoing throughout our effort to bring *who we are* and *what we do* into greater harmony. When we bring *who we are* and *what we do* into harmony, we become more *authentic* people. Remember, an *authentic* person is one who is trustworthy, honest, and real—one who does what he or she says and believes.

These processes are ever-present in life. I'm simply suggesting that these processes move through three developmental stages. Or at least, they can. It's up to you whether or not you will choose to experience all three stages of personal growth. You may choose to stay in the Mirrors stage, content with the prospect of only having to deal with the expectations of others and external influences. This is, admittedly, a safe place to be.

If you choose to move on to the Windows stage, you begin to move outside yourself as you begin creating, thinking, and valuing *who you think you can become.* With a sense of vision, your hopes and dreams become a more important part of *who you are.* This may naturally lead you to move through Windows to the Open Doors stage, where you become a person who is sincerely trying to make the world a better place by rendering service to other causes and people—not because that is the way you wish to be perceived, but because that is *who you are,* and that is what you value and believe. But again, only if you choose to.

All of this encompasses the dynamics of three constantly occurring interactions: *who others think I am, who I think I can become,* and *who I think I am.* While these three interactions change from stage to stage and their dominance shifts from one developmental level to the next, their interaction is constant. How we will respond to these interactions within us is, of course, up to us. Our choices will determine whether we are controlled by others or we interact with others in a positive, serving, interactive way.

Now, take out another piece of paper. Please answer, honestly and completely, the following questions:

1. Does what you've read within these pages offer direction to you for becoming a more *authentic* person?

    If your answer is "no," you have a couple of choices: (a) go back and study the book to see if you can find direction; or, (b) accept my thanks for reading the book and my encouragement to continue your personal search for authenticity.

2. If your answer is "yes," write a paragraph or two about how has this book influenced your thinking.

    For Example:

    -   Write a paragraph or two about how reading this book has led you to new thoughts about what you value, or caused you to take a look at what you value.

    -   Based on your analysis, write a paragraph or two about who you are right now.

    -   Write a paragraph or two committing yourself to what you are going to do to continue the process of becoming who you want to be.

Exercise Four

In Part Three we discussed five virtues that should be basic to guiding our behavior. These virtues—truth, gratitude, charity, self-discipline, and courage—are not new to our thinking. Most humans would agree that they are significant and valuable. The question is, do we really value these virtues individually and collectively, and is our behavior based upon them?

In this activity you will commit five days to studying these virtues and their application to your life.

Day One: The Virtue of Truth

On the first day, read Chapter Eight, "The Virtue of Truth," again. If you could read this the evening before it would give you more time to think about truth before Truth Day.

Following the pattern of diary-keeping established in Exercise One, record everything you see, hear or think that relates to truth. Do you see things that demonstrate truth or lack of truth in your everyday activities? Do you find examples of deception? Do you see or think of incidents when something could have or should have been said, but went unspoken?

At the end of the day find some quiet time to analyze your world from the perspective of truth. Write a page describing your feelings and thoughts. Do you find that you are filling your "empty self" with virtues more than the expectations of the world? Do you feel that you and the people with whom you associate are purposely working day-to-day toward greater use of the virtue of truth? Or do you find that life's pressures and the need to satisfy others still dominate your life?

From this experience, write two or three conclusions about truth as it relates to your life. From these conclusions, make one or two commitments to guide future behavior.

Day Two: The Virtue of Gratitude

This does not have to be a day directly following Day One. Choose a day during which you can focus on the next experience. On Day Two, or the evening just before, re-read Chapter Nine, "The Virtue of Gratitude." Follow the pattern outlined for Day One to study, feel and think about the virtue of gratitude as it applies to your life. Respond to the same set of question, as well as any others that occur to you while writing a one-page summary of you and the virtue of gratitude.

Day Three: The Virtue of Charity

Follow the same pattern as you did for Day One and Day Two.

Day Four: The Virtue of Self-Discipline

Follow the same pattern as you did for Days One, Two, and Three.

Day Five: The Virtue of Courage

Follow the same pattern as you did for Days One, Two, Three, and Four.

At the conclusion of Day Five, find some quiet, reflective time to sit and write about how congruent *who you are* (your virtue beliefs) is with *what you do*. Do the same for others (not necessarily individually, but collectively) you have observed during the five days.

From this experience, list some of the conclusions you have made about you and the five basic virtues. Based on these conclusions, write one or two commitments for future thoughts and actions in your process of becoming.

Exercise Five

In Part Four you read about serendipity, synergism and symbiosis. To analyze these important elements in your life, sit down for a few minutes with your diary or planner and do the following:

1. List five events in your lifetime that have been influenced by serendipity.

2. List five events in your life where the strength gained by a synergistic relationship has made the difference in happiness or unhappiness, or in success or failure.

3. List five events where you felt the power, warmth, and potential
    of symbiotic relationships.

From this exercise, write or dictate an "I Have a Dream" statement. "What if" you were becoming personally stronger in the ways we have discussed? "What if" you were forming synergistic relationships? "What if" those synergistic relationships joined together to form symbiotic relationships? "What if" your dream for yourself, your family, your community, and your work place—particularly as it relates to the concepts we have discussed—were to come true?

After you have written or taped your "I Have a Dream" statement, write another paragraph. In that paragraph, make a commitment to what you are going to do to make the dream come true.

Exercise Six

Write or dictate the speech you would like to have someone else give at your retirement dinner. This should reflect the thoughts and feelings you would like to have your family members and work associates say about you.

Then write or dictate another speech: the one that you would actually expect your family and associates to give about you if your retirement dinner were held today. When this is completed, identify the differences between the two speeches. From these differences make the necessary commitments to reach your own ideal for yourself. These commitments will provide a pretty good road map for you on your journey to authenticity.